SCHOOL ATLAS

AUTHOR Dr. Stephen Scoffham, Canterbury Christ Church University

CHIEF CONSULTANT Dr. David Lambert, Geographical Association

EDITORIAL CONSULTANTS Paul Baker, Alan Parkinson

The Publisher and author are grateful for additional support and advice from
Dr. Chris Young and other colleagues in the Department of Geographical and Life Sciences,
Canterbury Christ Church University.

DK

LONDON, NEW YORK, MELBOURNE, MUNICH, AND DELHI

Editor Jenny Finch
Art Editor Spencer Holbrook
DTP Designer Andy Hilliard
Editorial Assistant Steven Carton
Managing Cartographer David Roberts
Managing Editor Linda Esposito
Managing Art Editor Diane Thistlethwaite
Publishing Manager Andrew Macintyre
Category Publisher Laura Buller
Picture Researcher Kath Kollberg
Production Controller Lucy Baker
Jacket Designer Neil Cobourne
Jacket Editor Mariza O'Keeffe
US Editor Margaret Parrish

Original edition
Designer Clive Savage
Senior Cartographic Editor Simon Mumford
Cartographer Ed Merritt
Project Manager Nigel Duffield
DTP Designer David MacDonald

First published in the United States in 2007
by DK Publishing, 375 Hudson Street
New York, New York 10014

The contents of this atlas were originally published in Great Britain as the Longman School Atlas (2006)

DK books are available at special discounts when purchased in bulk for
sales promotions, premiums, fundraising, or educational use. For details, contact:
DK Publishing Special Markets, 375 Hudson Street
New York, New York 10014
SpecialSales@dk.com

A catalog record for this book is available from the Library of Congress.

ISBN: 978–0–7566–3270–0

Hi–res workflow proofed by MDP, UK
Printed and bound in Hong Kong

**Discover more at
www.dk.com**

CONTENTS

Key to map symbols

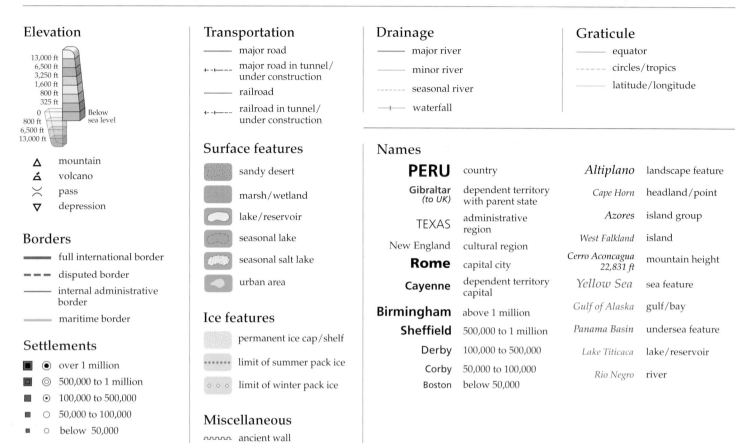

Elevation

13,000 ft
6,500 ft
3,250 ft
1,600 ft
800 ft
325 ft
0
800 ft — Below sea level
6,500 ft
13,000 ft

△ mountain
⩜ volcano
) (pass
▽ depression

Borders

▬▬▬ full international border
▬ ▬ ▬ disputed border
▬▬▬ internal administrative border
▬▬▬ maritime border

Settlements

■ ◉ over 1 million
▣ ◎ 500,000 to 1 million
■ ⊙ 100,000 to 500,000
■ ○ 50,000 to 100,000
■ ○ below 50,000

A red square indicates a national capital

Transportation

▬▬ major road
⊢⊣⊢⊣ major road in tunnel/ under construction
▬▬ railroad
⊢⊣⊢⊣ railroad in tunnel/ under construction

Surface features

sandy desert
marsh/wetland
lake/reservoir
seasonal lake
seasonal salt lake
urban area

Ice features

permanent ice cap/shelf
limit of summer pack ice
limit of winter pack ice

Miscellaneous

⌇⌇⌇⌇ ancient wall
● scientific station

Drainage

▬▬ major river
▬▬ minor river
┈┈┈ seasonal river
⊢|⊢ waterfall

Names

PERU country
Gibraltar (to UK) dependent territory with parent state
TEXAS administrative region
New England cultural region
Rome capital city
Cayenne dependent territory capital
Birmingham above 1 million
Sheffield 500,000 to 1 million
Derby 100,000 to 500,000
Corby 50,000 to 100,000
Boston below 50,000

Altiplano landscape feature
Cape Horn headland/point
Azores island group
West Falkland island
Cerro Aconcagua 22,831 ft mountain height
Yellow Sea sea feature
Gulf of Alaska gulf/bay
Panama Basin undersea feature
Lake Titicaca lake/reservoir
Rio Negro river

Graticule

▬▬ equator
▬▬ circles/tropics
▬▬ latitude/longitude

Key to map pages

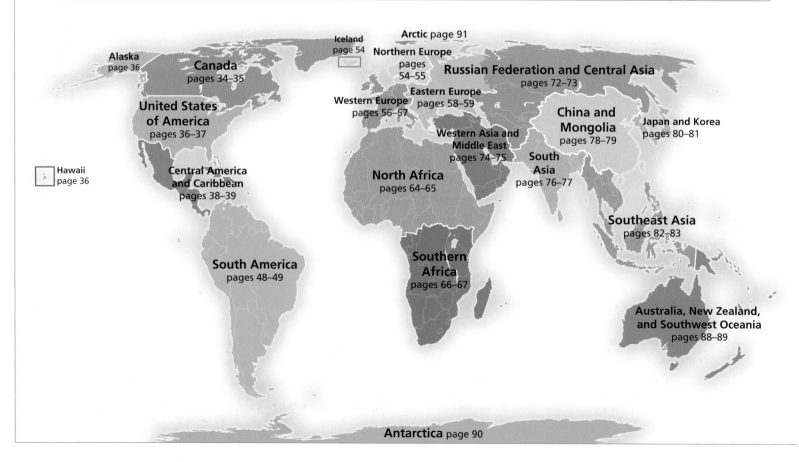

Alaska page 36
Canada pages 34–35
Iceland page 54
Arctic page 91
Northern Europe pages 54–55
Russian Federation and Central Asia pages 72–73
United States of America pages 36–37
Western Europe pages 56–57
Eastern Europe pages 58–59
China and Mongolia pages 78–79
Japan and Korea pages 80–81
Hawaii page 36
Central America and Caribbean pages 38–39
Western Asia and Middle East pages 74–75
South Asia pages 76–77
North Africa pages 64–65
South America pages 48–49
Southern Africa pages 66–67
Southeast Asia pages 82–83
Australia, New Zealand, and Southwest Oceania pages 88–89
Antarctica page 90

INTRODUCTION

An atlas is a book of maps. It tells you where places are and how they are connected. Atlases help us to explore different topics, such as climate, natural hazards, and population. In this way they tell us more about the world.

In addition to showing where places are, this atlas considers how places are changing. We live on a dynamic planet where water, air, and soil are always on the move. The way people interact with their surroundings and the environment also has an impact on the world. The problems associated with global warming are one aspect of a wider challenge—how can we live our lives without damaging the environment?

This atlas invites you to think about some of the main issues facing the world at the moment. The text, charts, diagrams, photographs, and satellite images provide extra information to help develop your ideas.

Using and drawing maps

The maps in this atlas aim to show the world as clearly and accurately as possible. In selecting and presenting information, the mapmaker has followed a number of rules. Check that you have followed this system when you draw any maps of your own.

Boundaries
All maps are drawn to the edge of the page, instead of fading away.

Latitude and longitude
Key lines of latitude and longitude are shown in blue.

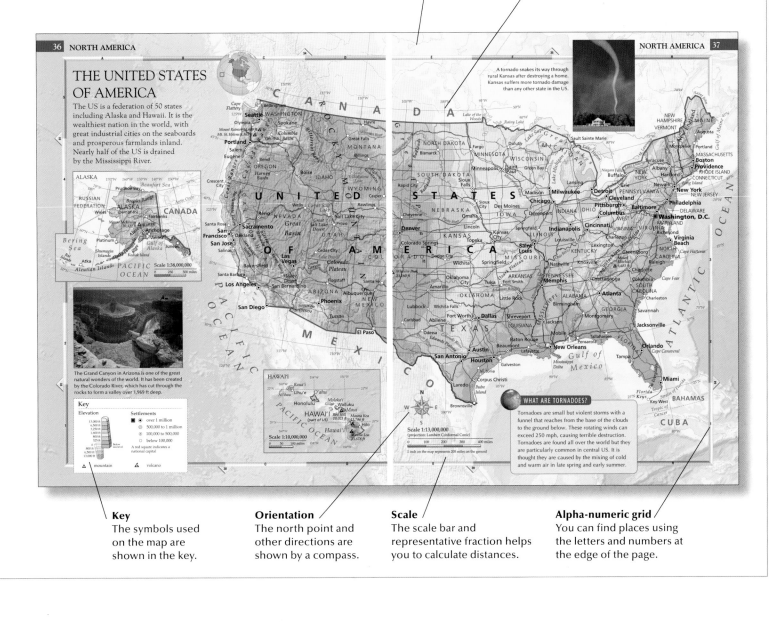

Key
The symbols used on the map are shown in the key.

Orientation
The north point and other directions are shown by a compass.

Scale
The scale bar and representative fraction helps you to calculate distances.

Alpha-numeric grid
You can find places using the letters and numbers at the edge of the page.

OUR WORLD

Sometimes it is important to describe exactly where places are on the earth's surface. Several thousand years ago, the Greeks and Romans developed a system of imaginary grid lines to solve this problem. This was the basis for the modern system of latitude and longitude.

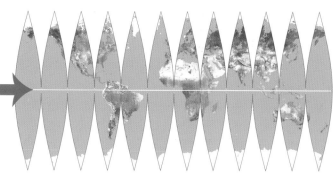

The only really accurate way to show the world is to use a globe. Flat maps always involve distortions but they do have the advantage of showing much more detail. Most of the maps in this atlas use the Eckert IV projection, which distorts area and direction as little as possible.

Latitude

Lines of latitude circle the earth, running parallel to each other from east to west. The most famous is the equator (0 degrees). The latitude of any place on the earth's surface is the angle between the place you want to describe, the equator, and the center of the earth. Latitude is measured in degrees north or south of the equator.

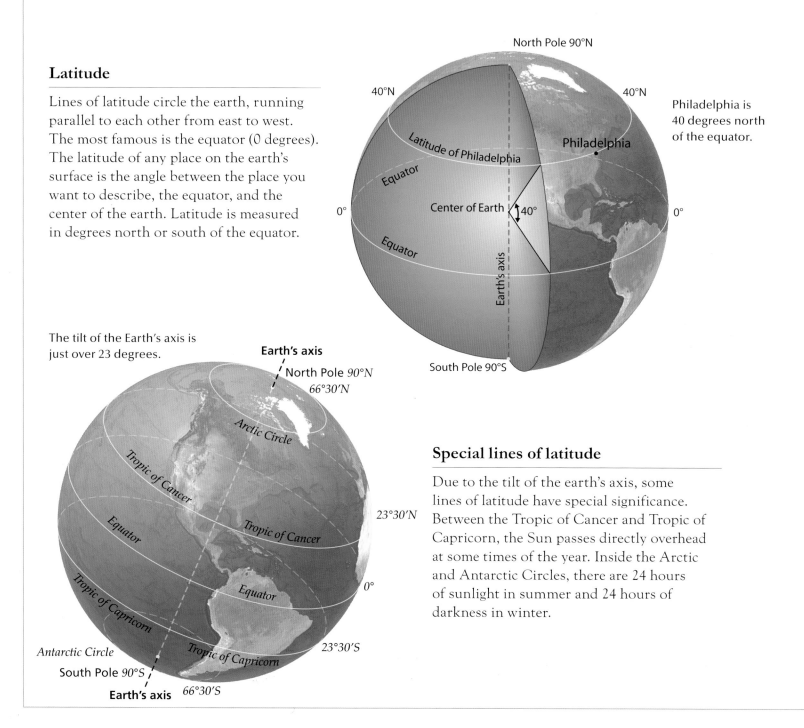

North Pole 90°N

40°N 40°N

Philadelphia is 40 degrees north of the equator.

Latitude of Philadelphia

Equator

Philadelphia

Center of Earth 40°

0° 0°

Equator

Earth's axis

South Pole 90°S

The tilt of the Earth's axis is just over 23 degrees.

Earth's axis
North Pole 90°N
66°30′N
Arctic Circle
Tropic of Cancer
Equator
Tropic of Cancer 23°30′N
Tropic of Capricorn
Equator 0°
Antarctic Circle 23°30′S
Tropic of Capricorn
South Pole 90°S
Earth's axis 66°30′S

Special lines of latitude

Due to the tilt of the earth's axis, some lines of latitude have special significance. Between the Tropic of Cancer and Tropic of Capricorn, the Sun passes directly overhead at some times of the year. Inside the Arctic and Antarctic Circles, there are 24 hours of sunlight in summer and 24 hours of darkness in winter.

Longitude

Lines of longitude run from north to south, dividing the world into segments. They are closest together at the poles and farthest apart at the equator. The longitude of any place is the angle between the Prime Meridian (0 degrees), the earth's axis, and the place you want to describe. Longitude is measured in degrees east or west of the Prime Meridian, which, by convention, passes through Greenwich in London.

North Pole 90°N

Prime Meridian

Earth's axis

Equator

30°E

Cairo

0°

Center of Earth

30°

0°

Equator

Longitude of Cairo

South Pole 90°S

Cairo is just over 30 degrees east of the Prime Meridian.

Time

Lines of longitude are important because they can be used to measure the spinning of the Earth, the basis for time. Places to the east of the Prime Meridian have an earlier sunrise than those to the west. The time changes exactly one hour for every 15 degrees of longitude. This explains why large countries are divided into time zones and why people who go on long journeys have to adjust their clocks.

International time zones

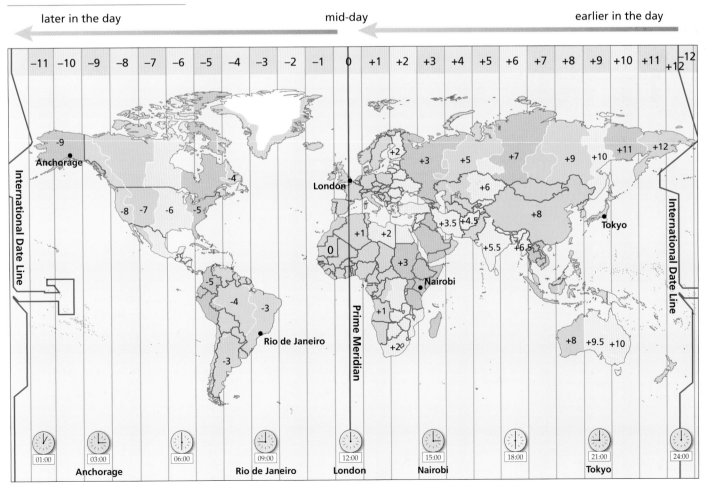

This map shows time differences around the world. At the international date line, the time changes by a full day.

POLITICAL

This map is called a political map because it shows different countries. At the moment there are almost 200 countries in the world, but the number of countries keeps changing as governments decide on different borders. Some borders follow physical features, such as rivers or mountain ranges. Others are long and straight because they follow lines of latitude or longitude. Borders often mark a change of language or culture.

What is a country?

All countries have a capital city, their own flag, and symbols to represent their identity. However, countries vary greatly in size ranging from small islands, like Sri Lanka, to vast territories, such as Canada and the Russian Federation.

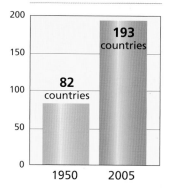

Number of countries

The break up of colonial empires around the world since 1950 has led to a huge increase in the number of countries.

Scale at equator 1:89,300,000
(projection: Eckert IV)

0   500   1,000   1,500   2,000   2,500 miles

1 inch on the map represents 1,409 miles on the ground

Key

Borders

——— international border

----- disputed border

——— maritime border

DISCUSSION

Which continent has the most countries?

How many countries do you think there might be in 50 years' time?

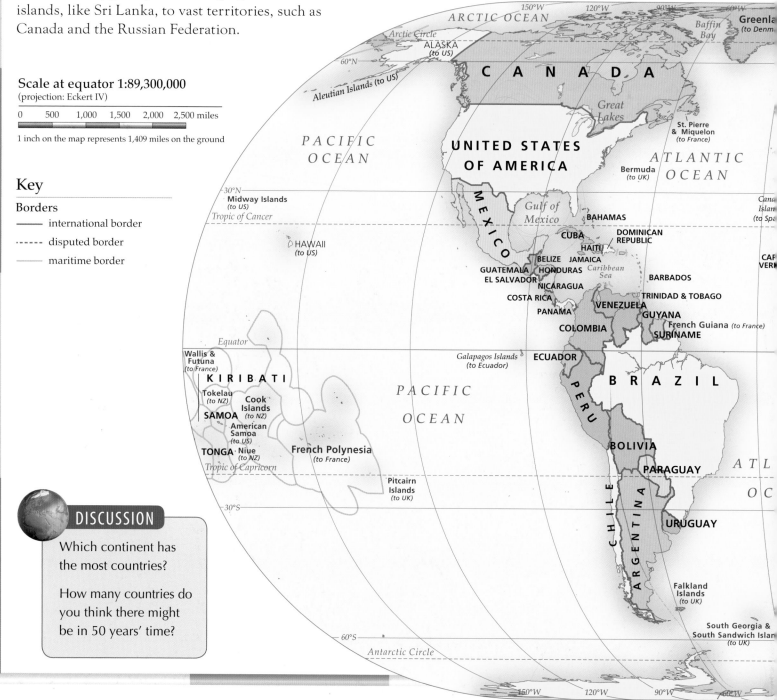

WEST AFRICA

WESTERN SAHARA (occupied by Morocco)
ALGERIA
LIBYA
Tropic of Cancer
MAURITANIA
MALI
NIGER
SENEGAL
GAMBIA
GUINEA-BISSAU
GUINEA
BURKINA FASO
SIERRA LEONE
CÔTE D'IVOIRE
GHANA
TOGO
BENIN
LIBERIA
NIGERIA
CAMEROON
EQUATORIAL GUINEA

Scale 1:45,000,000
0   250   500   750 miles

EUROPE

Faeroe Islands
NORWAY
SWEDEN
FINLAND
RUSSIAN FEDERATION
North Sea
UNITED KINGDOM
DENMARK
ESTONIA
LATVIA
RUSS. FED.
LITHUANIA
IRELAND
NETHERLANDS
GERMANY
POLAND
BELARUS
Channel Islands
BELGIUM
CZECH REPUBLIC
SLOVAKIA
UKRAINE
LUXEMBOURG
AUSTRIA
HUNGARY
MOLDOVA
SWITZERLAND
SLOVENIA
ROMANIA
FRANCE
CROATIA
BOSNIA & HERZEGOVINA
SERBIA
MONTENEGRO
BULGARIA
Caspian Sea
PORTUGAL
SPAIN
ITALY
MACEDONIA
ALBANIA
GREECE
TURKEY
Gibraltar
Mediterranean Sea
MALTA
CYPRUS

Scale 1:45,000,000
0   250   500   750 miles

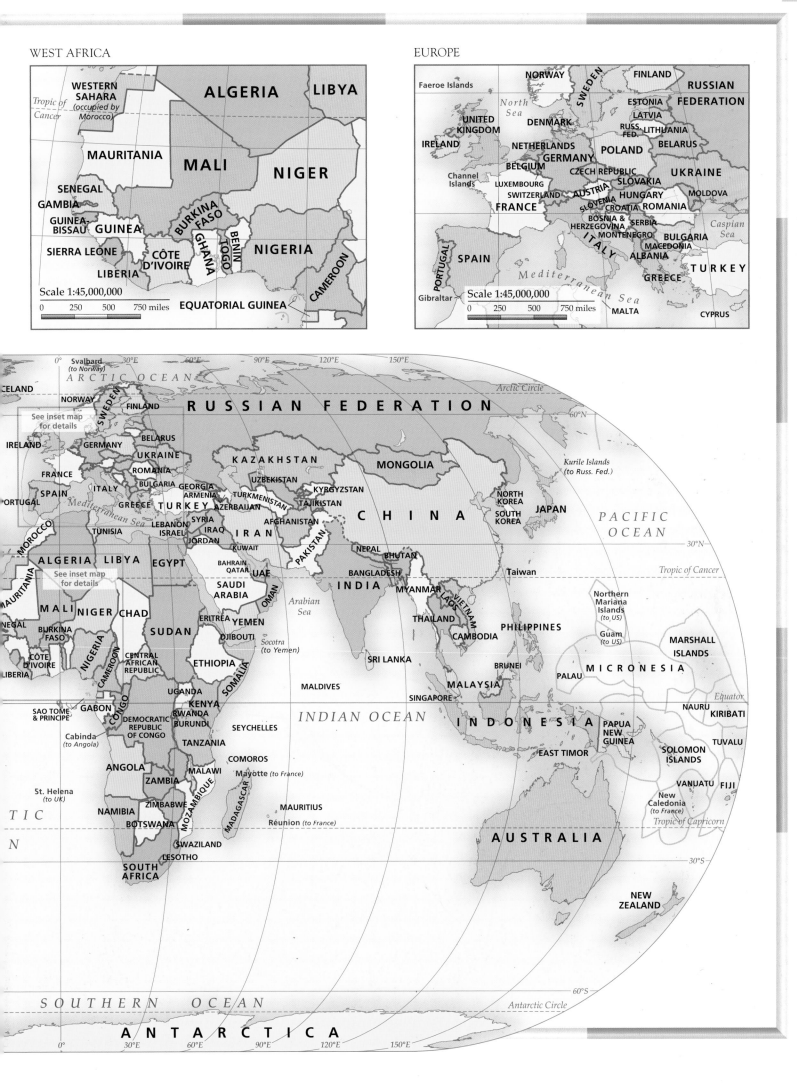

Svalbard (to Norway)
ARCTIC OCEAN
Arctic Circle
ICELAND
NORWAY
SWEDEN
FINLAND
RUSSIAN FEDERATION
60°N
See inset map for details
IRELAND
BELARUS
GERMANY
UKRAINE
KAZAKHSTAN
MONGOLIA
Kurile Islands (to Russ. Fed.)
FRANCE
ROMANIA
ITALY
BULGARIA
GEORGIA
ARMENIA
UZBEKISTAN
KYRGYZSTAN
NORTH KOREA
PORTUGAL
SPAIN
GREECE
TURKEY
AZERBAIJAN
TURKMENISTAN
TAJIKISTAN
CHINA
SOUTH KOREA
JAPAN
PACIFIC OCEAN
Mediterranean Sea
LEBANON
SYRIA
AFGHANISTAN
MOROCCO
TUNISIA
ISRAEL
IRAQ
JORDAN
IRAN
PAKISTAN
NEPAL
BHUTAN
Taiwan
30°N
KUWAIT
ALGERIA
LIBYA
EGYPT
BAHRAIN
QATAR
UAE
BANGLADESH
MYANMAR
Tropic of Cancer
See inset map for details
SAUDI ARABIA
OMAN
INDIA
LAOS
VIETNAM
Northern Mariana Islands (to US)
MAURITANIA
MALI
NIGER
CHAD
ERITREA
YEMEN
Arabian Sea
THAILAND
CAMBODIA
PHILIPPINES
Guam (to US)
MARSHALL ISLANDS
NEGAL
BURKINA FASO
SUDAN
DJIBOUTI
Socotra (to Yemen)
SRI LANKA
BRUNEI
MICRONESIA
CÔTE D'IVOIRE
NIGERIA
CAMEROON
CENTRAL AFRICAN REPUBLIC
ETHIOPIA
SOMALIA
MALDIVES
MALAYSIA
PALAU
LIBERIA
SAO TOME & PRINCIPE
GABON
CONGO
UGANDA
KENYA
SINGAPORE
INDONESIA
Equator
DEMOCRATIC REPUBLIC OF CONGO
RWANDA
BURUNDI
SEYCHELLES
INDIAN OCEAN
PAPUA NEW GUINEA
NAURU
KIRIBATI
Cabinda (to Angola)
TANZANIA
EAST TIMOR
SOLOMON ISLANDS
TUVALU
ANGOLA
MALAWI
COMOROS
Mayotte (to France)
St. Helena (to UK)
ZAMBIA
MOZAMBIQUE
MADAGASCAR
MAURITIUS
VANUATU
FIJI
New Caledonia (to France)
NAMIBIA
ZIMBABWE
Réunion (to France)
Tropic of Capricorn
TIC
BOTSWANA
AUSTRALIA
30°S
N
SWAZILAND
LESOTHO
SOUTH AFRICA
NEW ZEALAND
SOUTHERN OCEAN
Antarctic Circle
60°S
ANTARCTICA
0°   30°E   60°E   90°E   120°E   150°E

PHYSICAL

Almost two-thirds of the world's surface is covered by seas and oceans. The other third consists of islands and great blocks of land, known as continents.

What shapes the earth's surface?

Some parts of the earth are being lifted up into jagged mountain ranges. Other areas are being worn away by the action of rivers, ice, and the sea. The interaction between mountain building and erosion brings constant changes to the earth's surface.

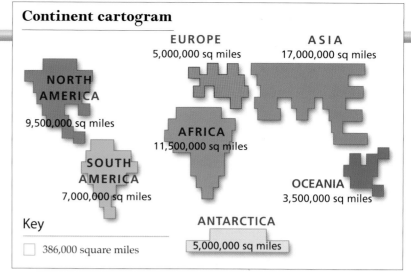

Continent cartogram

EUROPE
5,000,000 sq miles

ASIA
17,000,000 sq miles

NORTH AMERICA
9,500,000 sq miles

AFRICA
11,500,000 sq miles

SOUTH AMERICA
7,000,000 sq miles

OCEANIA
3,500,000 sq miles

ANTARCTICA
5,000,000 sq miles

Key

386,000 square miles

Instead of showing the shape of the coast, this map shows the area of each continent.

Key

Elevation

13,000 ft
6,500 ft
3,250 ft
1,600 ft
800 ft
325 ft
0
Below sea level
800 ft
6,500 ft
13,000 ft

△ mountain

▽ depression

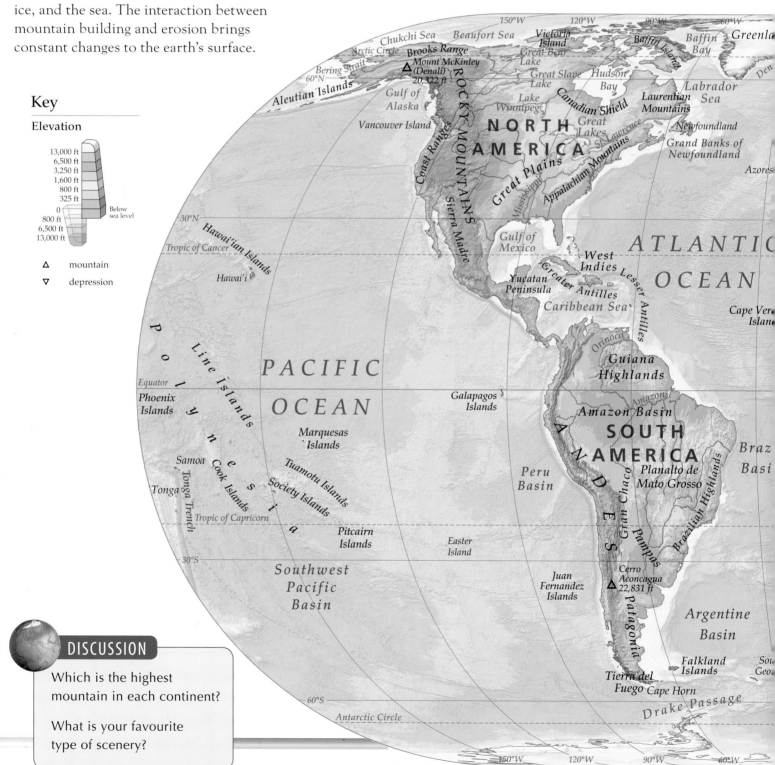

DISCUSSION

Which is the highest mountain in each continent?

What is your favourite type of scenery?

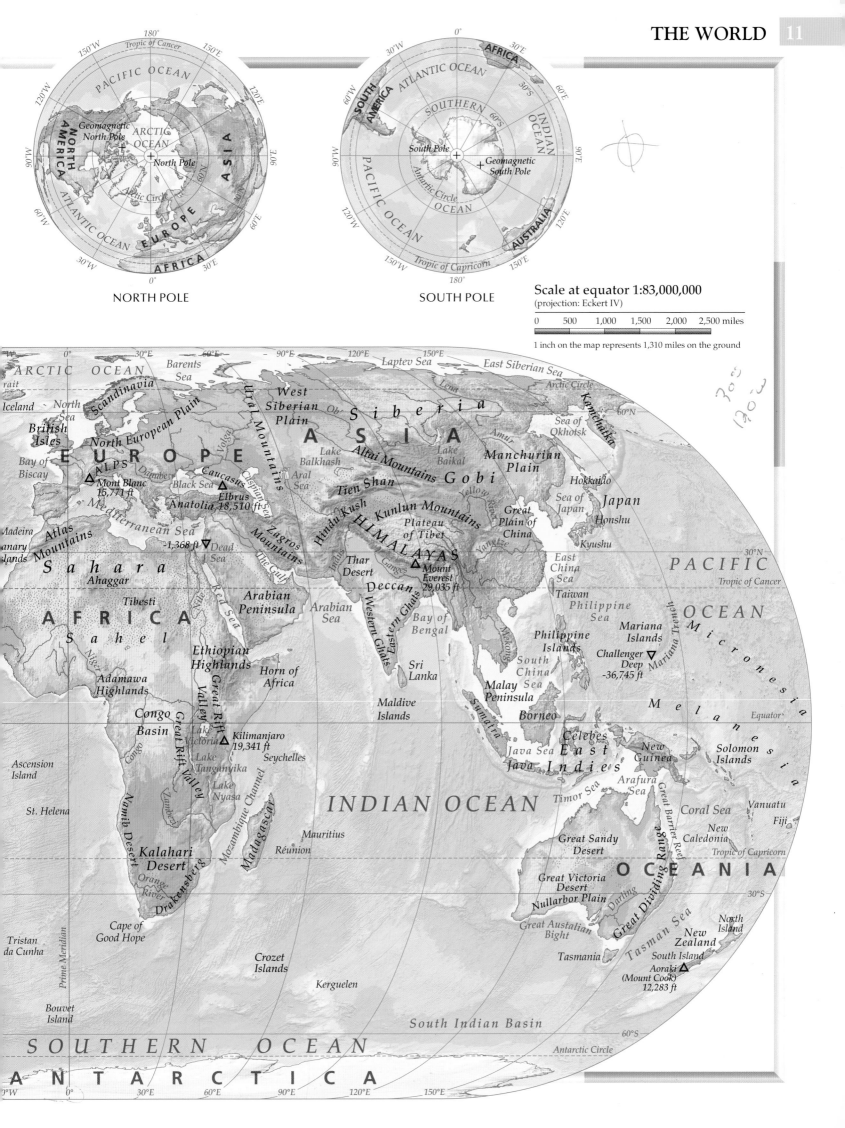

NORTH POLE

SOUTH POLE

Scale at equator 1:83,000,000
(projection: Eckert IV)

| 0 | 500 | 1,000 | 1,500 | 2,000 | 2,500 miles |

1 inch on the map represents 1,310 miles on the ground

North Pole map labels
PACIFIC OCEAN
Geomagnetic North Pole
North Pole
ARCTIC OCEAN
NORTH AMERICA
ASIA
EUROPE
ATLANTIC OCEAN
AFRICA
Arctic Circle
Tropic of Cancer
180° 150°W 150°E 120°W 120°E 90°W 90°E 60°W 60°E 30°W 30°E 0°

South Pole map labels
AFRICA
ATLANTIC OCEAN
SOUTH AMERICA
SOUTHERN OCEAN
INDIAN OCEAN
South Pole
Geomagnetic South Pole
Antarctic Circle
PACIFIC OCEAN
AUSTRALIA
Tropic of Capricorn
30°W 30°E 60°W 60°E 90°W 90°E 120°W 120°E 150°W 150°E 180° 0° 30°S 60°S

Main map
ARCTIC OCEAN
Barents Sea
Laptev Sea
East Siberian Sea
Arctic Circle
Iceland
North Sea
Scandinavia
West Siberian Plain
Siberia
Kamchatka
60°N
strait
British Isles
Bay of Biscay
EUROPE
North European Plain
Ural Mountains
Ob'
Lena
ASIA
Amur
Sea of Okhotsk
ALPS
Mont Blanc 15,771 ft
Danube
Volga
Lake Balkhash
Altai Mountains
Lake Baikal
Manchurian Plain
Hokkaido
Sea of Japan
Japan
Caucasus
Black Sea
Elbrus 18,510 ft
Anatolia
Caspian Sea
Aral Sea
Tien Shan
Gobi
Great Plain of China
Honshu
Atlas Mountains
Mediterranean Sea
Zagros Mountains
Hindu Kush
Kunlun Mountains
Plateau of Tibet
Yellow River
Kyushu
Madeira
Canary Islands
–1,368 ft Dead Sea
The Gulf
HIMALAYAS
Yangtze
East China Sea
PACIFIC OCEAN
30°N
Sahara
Ahaggar
Red Sea
Nile
Arabian Peninsula
Arabian Sea
Thar Desert
Ganges
Mount Everest 29,035 ft
Deccan
Taiwan
Tropic of Cancer
Tibesti
AFRICA
Western Ghats
Eastern Ghats
Bay of Bengal
Philippine Sea
Mariana Islands
Micronesia
Sahel
Ethiopian Highlands
Horn of Africa
Sri Lanka
Philippine Islands
OCEAN
Adamawa Highlands
Niger
Great Rift Valley
Maldive Islands
South China Sea
Challenger Deep –36,745 ft
Mariana Trench
Congo Basin
Lake Victoria
Kilimanjaro 19,341 ft
Malay Peninsula
Melanesia
Ascension Island
Congo
Great Rift Valley
Lake Tanganyika
Seychelles
Borneo
Sumatra
Celebes
New Guinea
Solomon Islands
Equator
St. Helena
Lake Nyasa
Java Sea
East Indies
Java
Namib Desert
Zambezi
Mozambique Channel
Madagascar
INDIAN OCEAN
Timor Sea
Arafura Sea
Great Barrier Reef
Coral Sea
New Caledonia
Vanuatu
Fiji
Kalahari Desert
Mauritius
Réunion
Great Sandy Desert
Great Dividing Range
Tropic of Capricorn
Orange River
Drakensberg
OCEANIA
Cape of Good Hope
Great Victoria Desert
Nullarbor Plain
Darling
Tristan da Cunha
Crozet Islands
Great Australian Bight
Tasman Sea
North Island
30°S
Bouvet Island
Kerguelen
Tasmania
New Zealand
South Island
Aoraki (Mount Cook) 12,283 ft
Prime Meridian
South Indian Basin
60°S
SOUTHERN OCEAN
Antarctic Circle
ANTARCTICA
0° 30°E 60°E 90°E 120°E 150°E

CLIMATE

There are great variations in weather across the earth's surface. Rain and temperature combine in different patterns according to the season. The average weather that affects a place over a number of years is called the climate.

Why do climates change?

The Sun provides the energy that drives the world's climate. Generally, the hottest places are near the equator where the Sun is overhead. By contrast, the coldest places are the polar regions where the Sun is always low in the sky. As the wind and ocean currents distribute the Sun's energy, different climates are created.

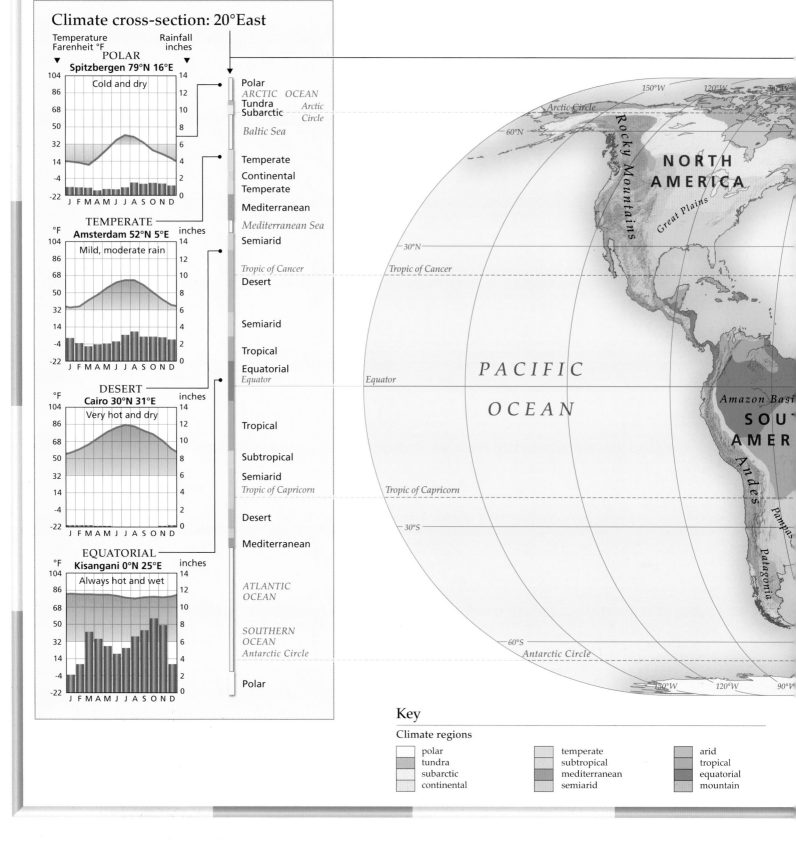

Climate cross-section: 20°East

Temperature Farenheit °F — Rainfall inches

POLAR
Spitzbergen 79°N 16°E
Cold and dry

TEMPERATE
Amsterdam 52°N 5°E
Mild, moderate rain

DESERT
Cairo 30°N 31°E
Very hot and dry

EQUATORIAL
Kisangani 0°N 25°E
Always hot and wet

Polar
ARCTIC OCEAN
Tundra
Subarctic — Arctic Circle
Baltic Sea
Temperate
Continental
Temperate
Mediterranean
Mediterranean Sea
Semiarid
Tropic of Cancer
Desert
Semiarid
Tropical
Equatorial
Equator
Tropical
Subtropical
Semiarid
Tropic of Capricorn
Desert
Mediterranean
ATLANTIC OCEAN
SOUTHERN OCEAN
Antarctic Circle
Polar

Key

Climate regions

polar	temperate	arid
tundra	subtropical	tropical
subarctic	mediterranean	equatorial
continental	semiarid	mountain

NORTH AMERICA
Rocky Mountains
Great Plains
PACIFIC OCEAN
Amazon Basin
SOUTH AMERICA
Andes
Pampas
Patagonia

Arctic Circle
60°N
30°N
Tropic of Cancer
Equator
Tropic of Capricorn
30°S
60°S
Antarctic Circle
150°W 120°W

Ocean currents move heat around the world. This satellite image shows the temperature of surface water in May. Note especially the cold current on the west coast of South America and the relatively warm seas around the UK.

— Climate cross-section: 20°East

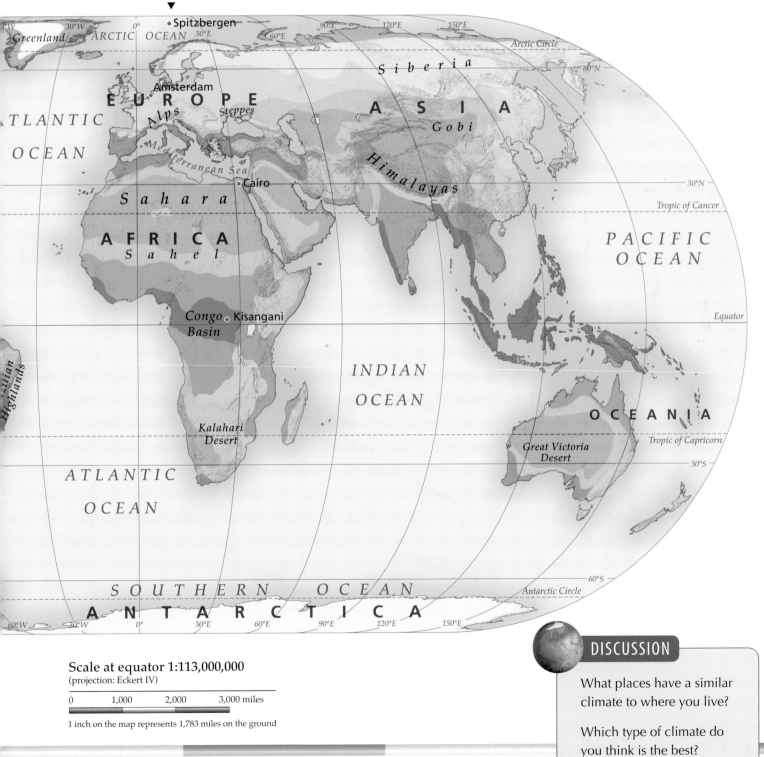

Scale at equator 1:113,000,000
(projection: Eckert IV)

0   1,000   2,000   3,000 miles

1 inch on the map represents 1,783 miles on the ground

DISCUSSION

What places have a similar climate to where you live?

Which type of climate do you think is the best?

CLIMATE CHANGE

The evidence from plants, ice cores, rocks, and soils shows that the earth's climate is always changing. At different times in the past, the earth has been both much warmer and much colder than it is today. These changes can happen gradually over thousands of years or rapidly over a few decades.

What is global warming?

Scientists are now convinced that the world's climate is getting warmer. They have detected a steady increase in the amount of carbon dioxide and other gases in the atmosphere that trap the heat of the Sun. Some nations regard global warming as a very serious threat and have signed the Kyoto Agreement to stabilize and eventually lower air pollution levels.

Greenhouse gases

Carbon dioxide levels
(parts per million)

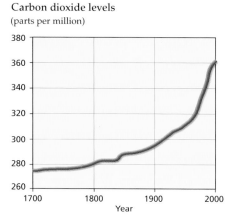

Carbon dioxide is a main cause of global warming. The quantity of carbon dioxide in the atmosphere has increased steadily since the Industrial Revolution in 1850. Levels are expected to continue to increase.

The impact of global warming

It is impossible to predict exactly how fast temperatures will rise and how global warming will affect us. The map and text boxes show some of the possibilities.

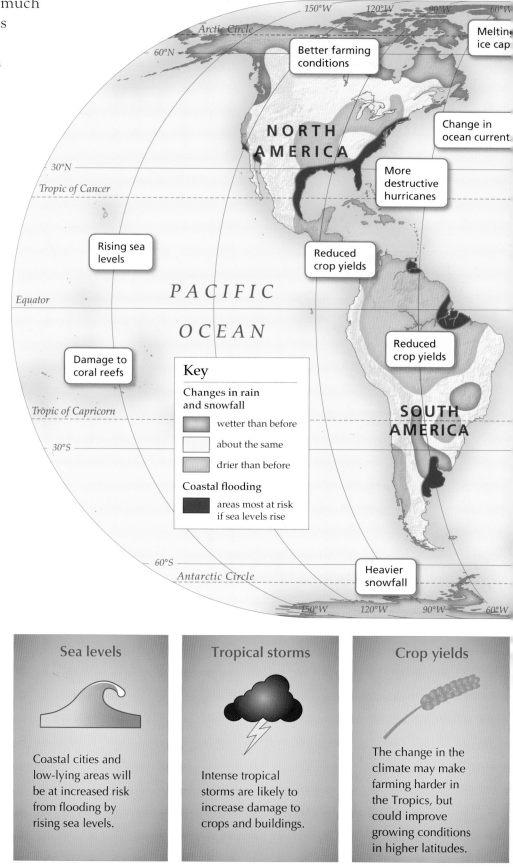

Better farming conditions

Melting ice cap

Change in ocean current

More destructive hurricanes

Rising sea levels

Reduced crop yields

NORTH AMERICA

Damage to coral reefs

Reduced crop yields

SOUTH AMERICA

Heavier snowfall

PACIFIC OCEAN

Key

Changes in rain and snowfall
- wetter than before
- about the same
- drier than before

Coastal flooding
- areas most at risk if sea levels rise

Arctic Circle
60°N
30°N
Tropic of Cancer
Equator
Tropic of Capricorn
30°S
60°S
Antarctic Circle
150°W   120°W   90°W   60°W

Sea levels

Coastal cities and low-lying areas will be at increased risk from flooding by rising sea levels.

Tropical storms

Intense tropical storms are likely to increase damage to crops and buildings.

Crop yields

The change in the climate may make farming harder in the Tropics, but could improve growing conditions in higher latitudes.

Global warming *"is the most serious threat that humanity has faced in all its recorded history."*

Lord May, leading UK scientist

Scale at equator 1:113,000,000
(projection: Eckert IV)

0	1,000	2,000	3,000 miles

1 inch on the map represents 1,783 miles on the ground

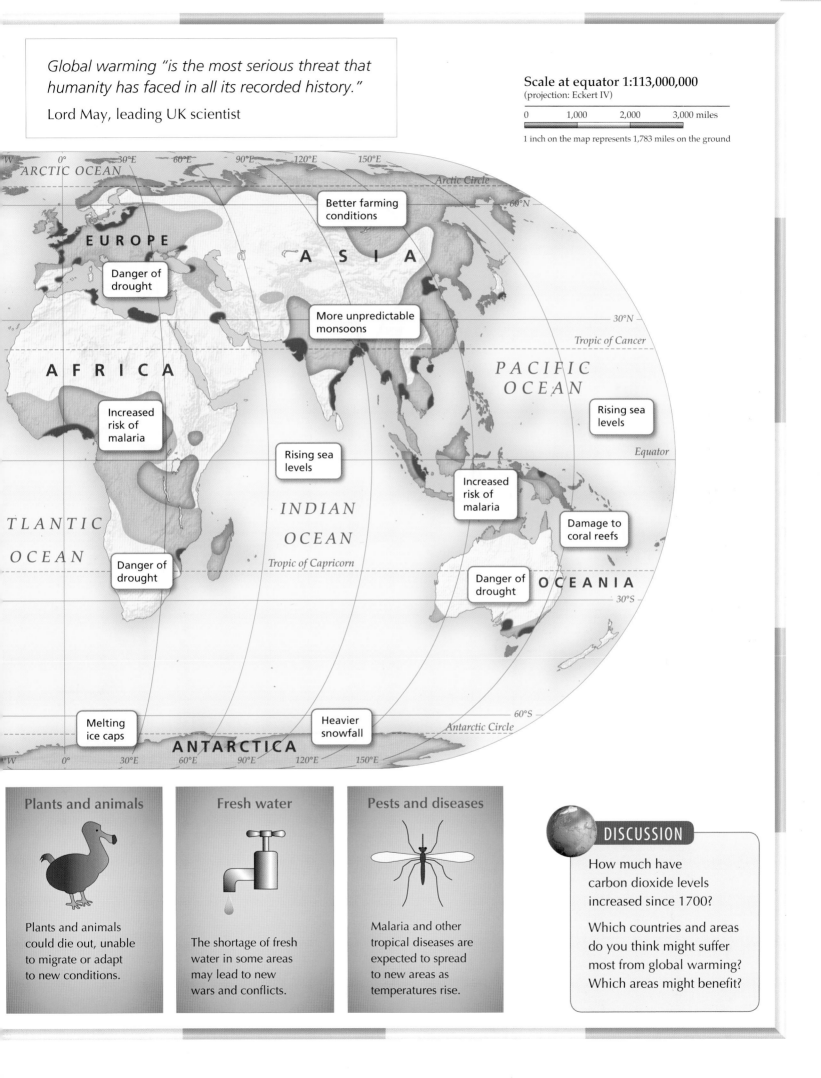

ARCTIC OCEAN

Arctic Circle

EUROPE

ASIA

Better farming conditions

Danger of drought

More unpredictable monsoons

30°N

Tropic of Cancer

AFRICA

PACIFIC OCEAN

Increased risk of malaria

Rising sea levels

Rising sea levels

Equator

INDIAN OCEAN

Increased risk of malaria

ATLANTIC OCEAN

Damage to coral reefs

Tropic of Capricorn

Danger of drought

Danger of drought

OCEANIA

30°S

Melting ice caps

Heavier snowfall

Antarctic Circle

60°S

ANTARCTICA

60°N

Plants and animals

Plants and animals could die out, unable to migrate or adapt to new conditions.

Fresh water

The shortage of fresh water in some areas may lead to new wars and conflicts.

Pests and diseases

Malaria and other tropical diseases are expected to spread to new areas as temperatures rise.

DISCUSSION

How much have carbon dioxide levels increased since 1700?

Which countries and areas do you think might suffer most from global warming? Which areas might benefit?

NATURAL DISASTERS

Violent or unexpected changes often happen to the earth's surface. When they kill people they are known as natural disasters. Natural disasters include droughts, floods, storms, earthquakes, and volcanic eruptions. As the world population grows larger, deaths and damage from natural disasters are increasing. However, better communications are making us more aware of the risks.

Volcanoes

The molten rock deep within the earth breaks out onto the surface in volcanoes. Many volcanoes are harmless, but when they erupt the force can devastate large areas and poisonous gas spreads high into the sky.

Earthquakes

Earthquakes happen when the different parts of the earth's crust collide, slide into each other, or tear apart. When the epicenter is near a town or city many people can be killed. If the earthquake sets off a tsunami, or tidal wave, it can cause even more damage.

This series of photographs shows what happened in less than a minute when Mount St. Helens erupted on May 18, 1980.

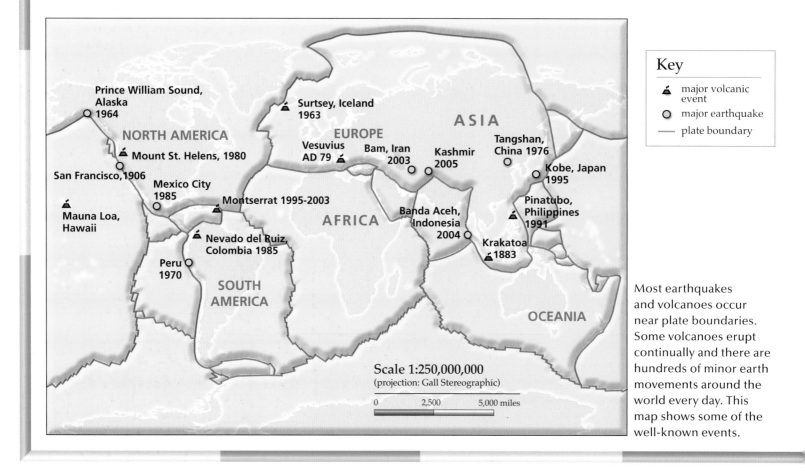

Prince William Sound, Alaska
○ 1964

Surtsey, Iceland
▲ 1963

ASIA

NORTH AMERICA

EUROPE
Vesuvius
AD 79 ▲

Bam, Iran
2003

Kashmir
2005 ○

Tangshan,
China 1976
○

▲ Mount St. Helens, 1980

Kobe, Japan
○ 1995

San Francisco, 1906 ○

Mexico City
1985
○

Montserrat 1995-2003 ▲

Pinatubo,
Philippines
▲ 1991

▲
Mauna Loa,
Hawaii

AFRICA

Banda Aceh,
Indonesia
2004 ○

▲ Nevado del Ruiz,
Colombia 1985

Krakatoa
▲ 1883

Peru ○
1970

**SOUTH
AMERICA**

OCEANIA

Key
▲ major volcanic event
○ major earthquake
— plate boundary

Scale 1:250,000,000
(projection: Gall Stereographic)

0   2,500   5,000 miles

Most earthquakes and volcanoes occur near plate boundaries. Some volcanoes erupt continually and there are hundreds of minor earth movements around the world every day. This map shows some of the well-known events.

Droughts

Long periods with very little rain are known as droughts. Trees and plants shrivel without water and people and animals struggle to get enough to drink. Sometimes the desert spreads over the parched land, increasing the damage.

Tropical storms

In the Tropics, the warmth of the sea causes severe storms to develop at certain times of the year. Devastating winds and torrential rain can destroy whole communities and people are killed as buildings collapse.

Floods

Heavy rain, tidal waves, and earthquakes all cause floods. If people are given enough warning they may be able to escape, but houses and crops will still be ruined.

Tropical storm tracks

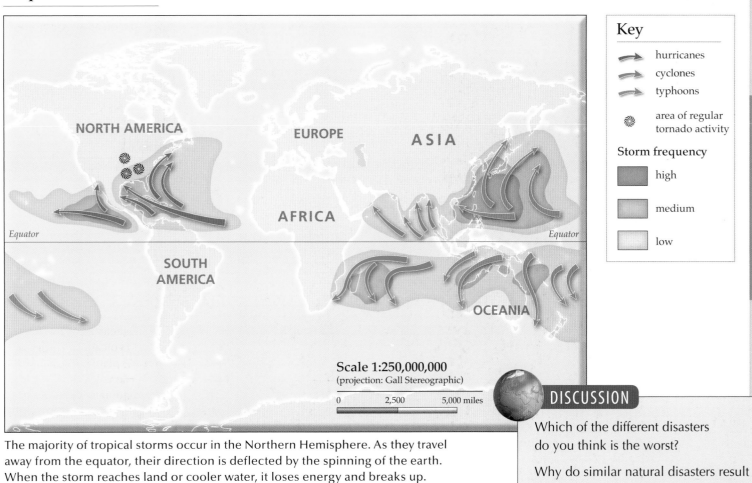

Key

- ➤ hurricanes
- ➤ cyclones
- ➤ typhoons
- 🌀 area of regular tornado activity

Storm frequency

- high
- medium
- low

Scale 1:250,000,000
(projection: Gall Stereographic)

0   2,500   5,000 miles

NORTH AMERICA · EUROPE · ASIA · AFRICA · SOUTH AMERICA · OCEANIA · Equator

The majority of tropical storms occur in the Northern Hemisphere. As they travel away from the equator, their direction is deflected by the spinning of the earth. When the storm reaches land or cooler water, it loses energy and breaks up.

DISCUSSION

Which of the different disasters do you think is the worst?

Why do similar natural disasters result in very different amounts of damage?

LIFE ON EARTH

Different areas of the earth have a unique
combination of climate, plants, and scenery.
These are known as biomes. Some biomes,
such as tropical rain forests, have a huge variety
of plants and creatures. Other biomes such as
grasslands and deciduous forests have been
greatly altered by human activity.

Rocky mountains, Wyoming

Sahara Desert, Libya, North Africa

Key

World biomes

- polar
- tundra
- coniferous forest
- deciduous forest
- grassland
- mediterranean
- savanna
- tropical forest
- hot desert
- cold desert
- mountain

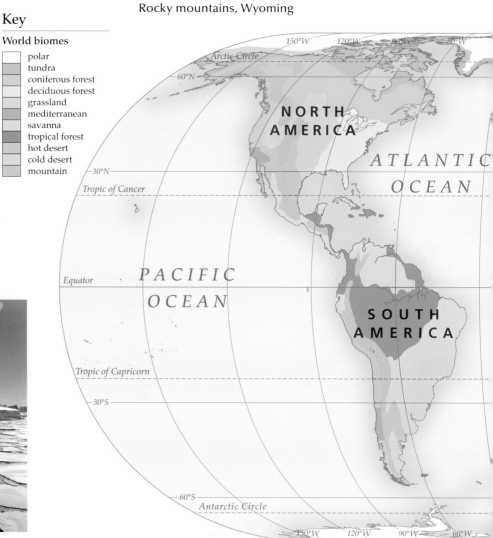

Pack ice and icebergs, Arctic Ocean

Eastern Siberia,
Russian Federation

Scale at equator 1:150,000,000
(projection: Eckert IV)

| 0 | 1,000 | 2,000 | 3,000 | 4,000 mile |

1 inch on the map represents 2,368 miles
on the ground

Grassland

Pampas grass, Argentina

Flagship species

Scientists believe that half of all plant and animal species could become extinct in the next 50 years. Conservation groups are focusing their campaigns on a few flagship species that, as well as being at risk themselves, provide an "umbrella" for other forms of wildlife.

Flagship species include:

Giant pandas

Tigers

Whales/dolphins

Rhinos

Elephants

Turtles

Great apes

AT RISK

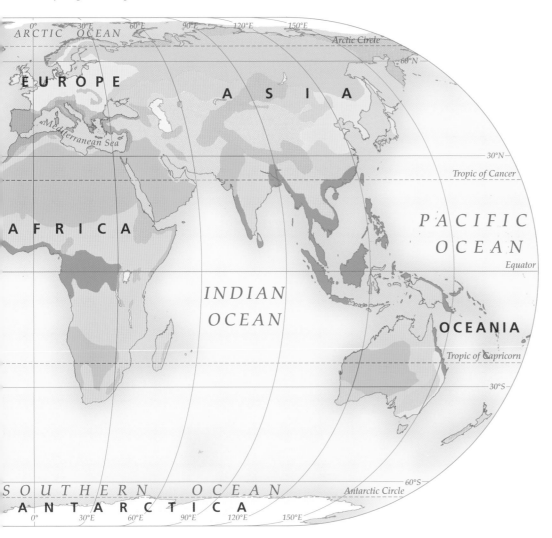

Deciduous forest

Burnham Beeches, Buckinghamshire, UK

Tropical rain forest

Rancho Grande, Venezuela, South America

Savanna

Tarangire National Park, Tanzania, East Africa

DISCUSSION

Which parts of the world have the same biome as your area?

Can human activity ever improve a biome?

THREATENED ENVIRONMENTS

The environment has suffered as people use the earth's resources for industry, farming, and leisure. Pollution and the loss of plant and animal life are now widespread.

Rain forests

Around the world forests are shrinking as trees are cut for lumber and land is cleared for farming. In Europe, the temperate forests were cut down centuries ago. The rain forests, which are home to a great number of different plants and creatures, are now particularly at risk.

Key

Disappearing forests

- existing rain forest
- destroyed rain forest

Desertification

Around the world dry areas are becoming deserts as people put more and more pressure on the land. Climate change, overgrazing, and clearing wood for firewood are all making the problem worse.

Key

Spreading deserts

- existing desert
- high risk of desertification
- medium risk of desertification

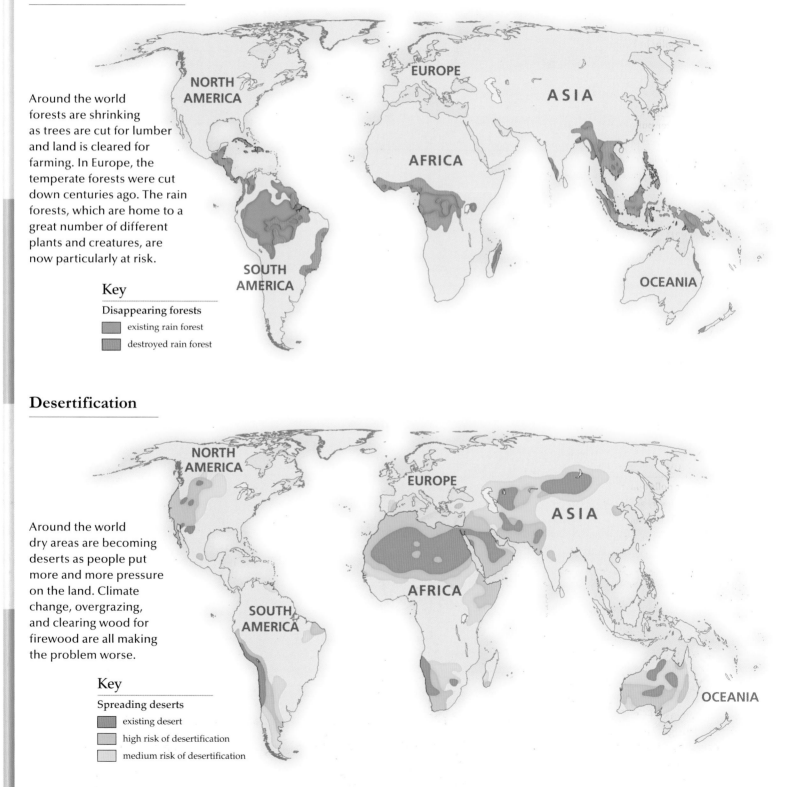

Water pollution

Pollution affects many rivers, seas, and oceans. Some coastlines are being damaged by waste from factories, farms, and cities. Oil pollution is another problem, especially in busy shipping lanes.

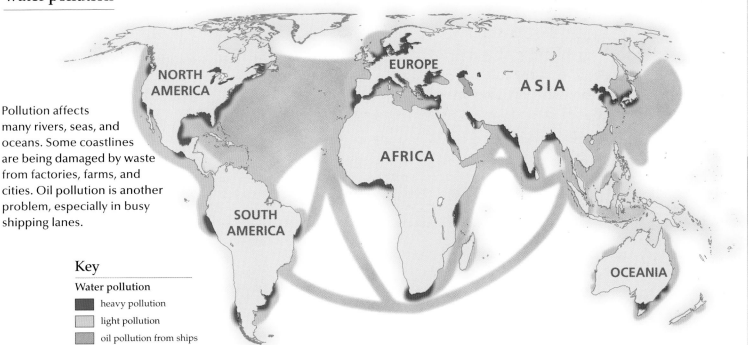

Key

Water pollution

- heavy pollution
- light pollution
- oil pollution from ships

Air pollution

Acid rain is caused by the sulfur and nitrogen that is released from burning coal, oil, and gas. The acid can kill trees and plants as well as fish in rivers and lakes.

Key

Air pollution

- very acidic rain
- acid rain
- slightly acidic rain
- areas with polluted air
- areas that may have problems in the future

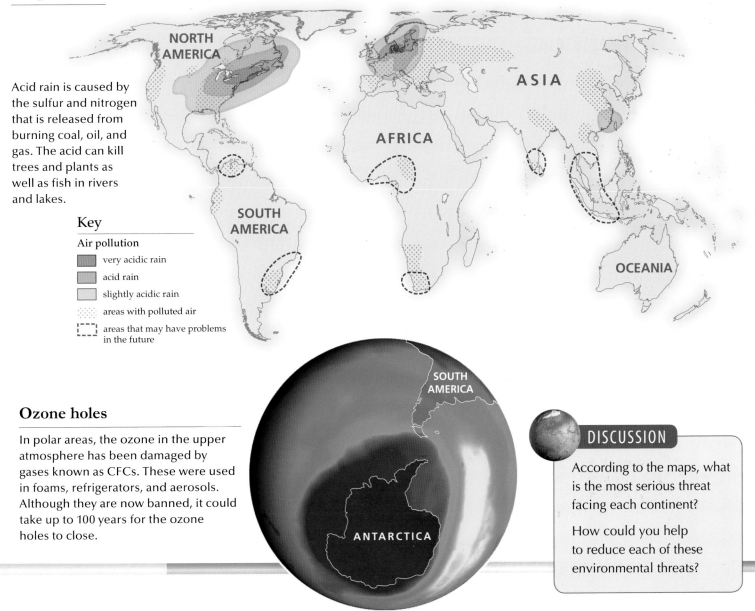

Ozone holes

In polar areas, the ozone in the upper atmosphere has been damaged by gases known as CFCs. These were used in foams, refrigerators, and aerosols. Although they are now banned, it could take up to 100 years for the ozone holes to close.

DISCUSSION

According to the maps, what is the most serious threat facing each continent?

How could you help to reduce each of these environmental threats?

POPULATION

The number of people in the world has tripled in the last 100 years. Numbers are expected to continue to rise throughout this century. However, the rate of increase will slow down and some regions, such as southeast Europe, may actually become emptier.

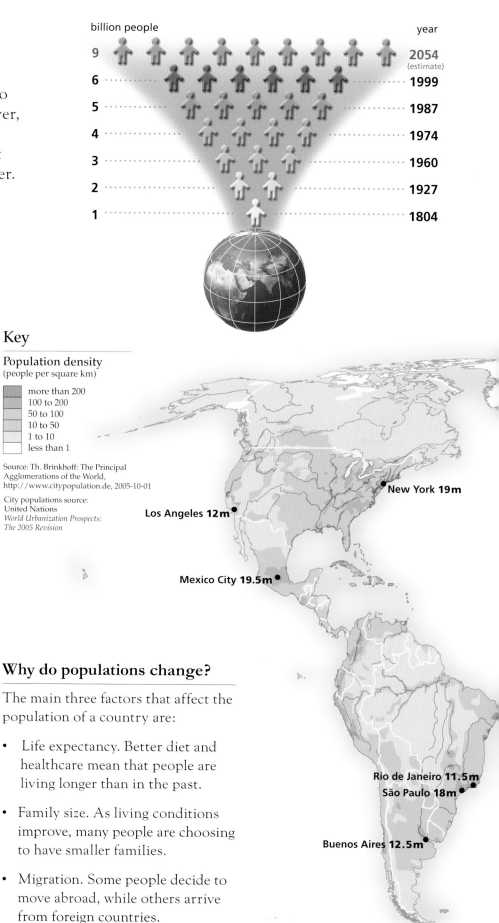

billion people

	year
9	2054 (estimate)
6	1999
5	1987
4	1974
3	1960
2	1927
1	1804

World's most populous countries: 2005

Population (millions)

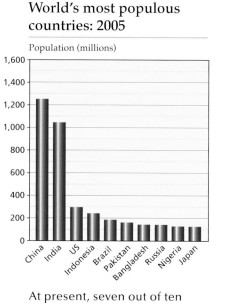

China, India, US, Indonesia, Brazil, Pakistan, Bangladesh, Russia, Nigeria, Japan

At present, seven out of ten of the world's most populous countries are in Asia.

World's most populous countries: 2050

Population (millions)

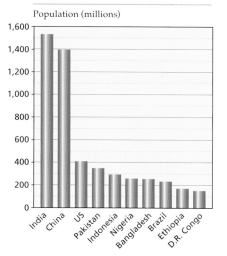

India, China, US, Pakistan, Indonesia, Nigeria, Bangladesh, Brazil, Ethiopia, D.R. Congo

By 2050 the population of countries in south Asia and parts of central Africa will have grown considerably.

Key

Population density
(people per square km)

- more than 200
- 100 to 200
- 50 to 100
- 10 to 50
- 1 to 10
- less than 1

Source: Th. Brinkhoff: The Principal Agglomerations of the World, http://www.citypopulation.de, 2005-10-01

City populations source:
United Nations
*World Urbanization Prospects:
The 2005 Revision*

Why do populations change?

The main three factors that affect the population of a country are:

- Life expectancy. Better diet and healthcare mean that people are living longer than in the past.

- Family size. As living conditions improve, many people are choosing to have smaller families.

- Migration. Some people decide to move abroad, while others arrive from foreign countries.

New York 19m
Los Angeles 12m
Mexico City 19.5m
Rio de Janeiro 11.5m
São Paulo 18m
Buenos Aires 12.5m

Population cartogram

This cartogram shows countries according to their population. It is possible to compare the number of people without thinking about the size of the country.

Key

Country area proportional to population

- 1 million people

EUROPE

Russian Federation 143 million

United Kingdom 60 million

NORTH AMERICA

Canada 33 million

United States of America 298 million

Germany 84 million

France 60 million

Italy 58 million

Spain 40 million

China 1.31 billion

ASIA

Turkey 70 million

Iran 68 million

Pakistan 166 million

India 1.09 billion

Japan 128 million

South Korea 48 million

Vietnam 84 million

Philippines 89 million

Cuba 11 million

Mexico 107 million

Venezuela 25 million

Colombia 44 million

Morocco 33 million

Egypt 79 million

Nigeria 132 million

Bangladesh 147 million

Peru 28 million

Brazil 188 million

Ethiopia 75 million

Indonesia 245 million

AFRICA

Tanzania 37 million

Argentina 39 million

SOUTH AMERICA

South Africa 45 million

Australia 20 million

OCEANIA

Moscow 10.5m

London 8.5m

Istanbul 10m

Tehran 7m

Cairo 11m

Karachi 11.6m

Delhi 15m

Beijing 12m

Seoul 9.6m

Tokyo 35m

Osaka 11m

Shanghai 14.5m

Dhaka 12.5m

Kolkata 14m

Shenzhen 7m

Mumbai 18m

Manila 10.7m

Lagos 11m

Jakarta 13m

Scale at equator 1:99,700,000
(projection: Eckert IV)

| 0 | 1,000 | 2,000 | 3,000 miles |

1 inch on the map represents 1,574 miles on the ground

DISCUSSION

Which two continents have the smallest populations (aside from Antarctica)?

How might an increase or decrease in population affect a country?

GLOBALIZATION

The world is linked together by patterns of trade and communication. These links mean that many of the things that we use or see in the stores are imported from other countries. Over the past few decades, there has been a huge increase in the exchange of goods, services, and technology around the world. This process is known as globalization.

World air transportation

People have been traveling to far-flung parts of the world for thousands of years. Today, air transportation makes international travel easy, but this comes at a high price environmentally. Many of the world's most heavily trafficked routes are internal US flights.

Trade power

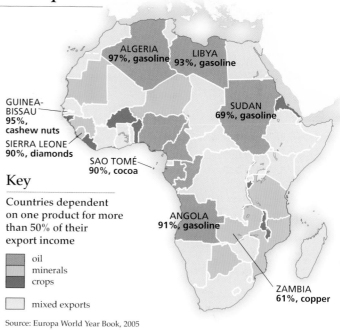

Key

Countries dependent on one product for more than 50% of their export income

- oil
- minerals
- crops
- mixed exports

Source: Europa World Year Book, 2005

Many African countries earn more than half their export income from just one product, such as gas or metal ore. This makes them very vulnerable to price changes and unexpected events.

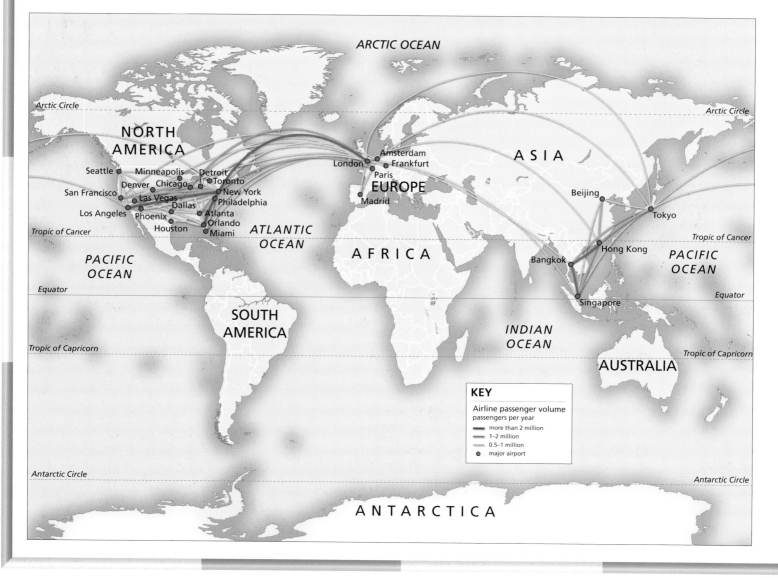

KEY

Airline passenger volume
passengers per year
- more than 2 million
- 1–2 million
- 0.5–1 million
- major airport

Why has globalization happened?

Globalization allows companies to take advantage of resources, skills, and cheaper labor costs in LEDCs (see page 92). It also means people can eat fruit and vegetables even when they are out of season. The expansion of air travel and the development of the Internet have made global communications easier than ever before. This too has helped to bind countries together.

World computer

Computers are made from lots of different parts. The map below provides information about an American company. The computers that it sells are made from parts that come from all over the world. Altogether about 400 companies are involved in supplying components. Many of these are in Asia.

Transnational companies (TNCs) are huge businesses that operate in many countries around the world. Some TNCs help to develop the country's economy, whilst others can exploit low-paid workers.

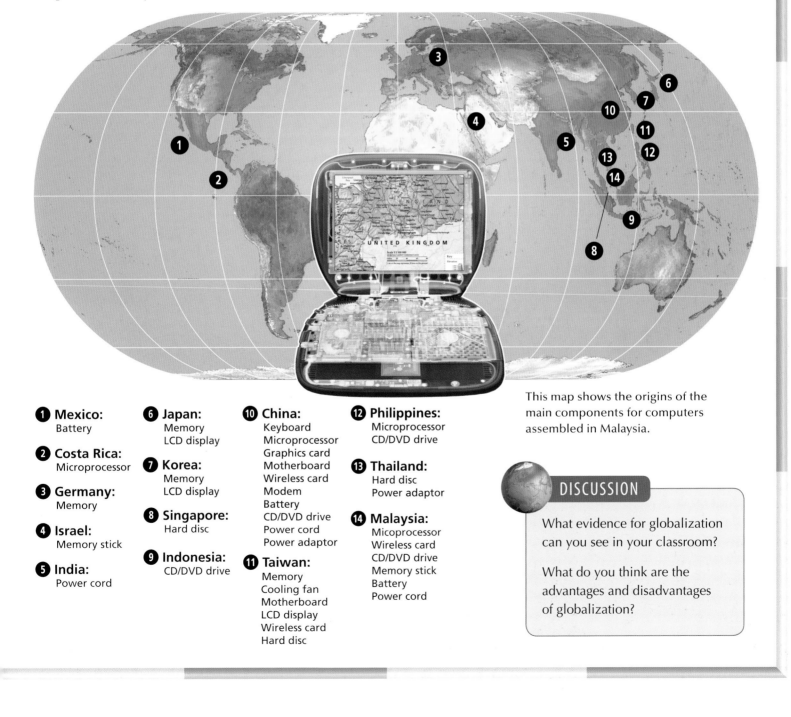

This map shows the origins of the main components for computers assembled in Malaysia.

1 Mexico:
Battery

2 Costa Rica:
Microprocessor

3 Germany:
Memory

4 Israel:
Memory stick

5 India:
Power cord

6 Japan:
Memory
LCD display

7 Korea:
Memory
LCD display

8 Singapore:
Hard disc

9 Indonesia:
CD/DVD drive

10 China:
Keyboard
Microprocessor
Graphics card
Motherboard
Wireless card
Modem
Battery
CD/DVD drive
Power cord
Power adaptor

11 Taiwan:
Memory
Cooling fan
Motherboard
LCD display
Wireless card
Hard disc

12 Philippines:
Microprocessor
CD/DVD drive

13 Thailand:
Hard disc
Power adaptor

14 Malaysia:
Micoprocessor
Wireless card
CD/DVD drive
Memory stick
Battery
Power cord

DISCUSSION

What evidence for globalization can you see in your classroom?

What do you think are the advantages and disadvantages of globalization?

NORTH AMERICA POLITICAL

North America is dominated by the United States, the world's most powerful nation. Canada and Mexico are the two other largest countries. To the south, there are the islands of the Caribbean and the narrow neck of land in Central America, which is divided into many smaller nations.

Key

■ capital city

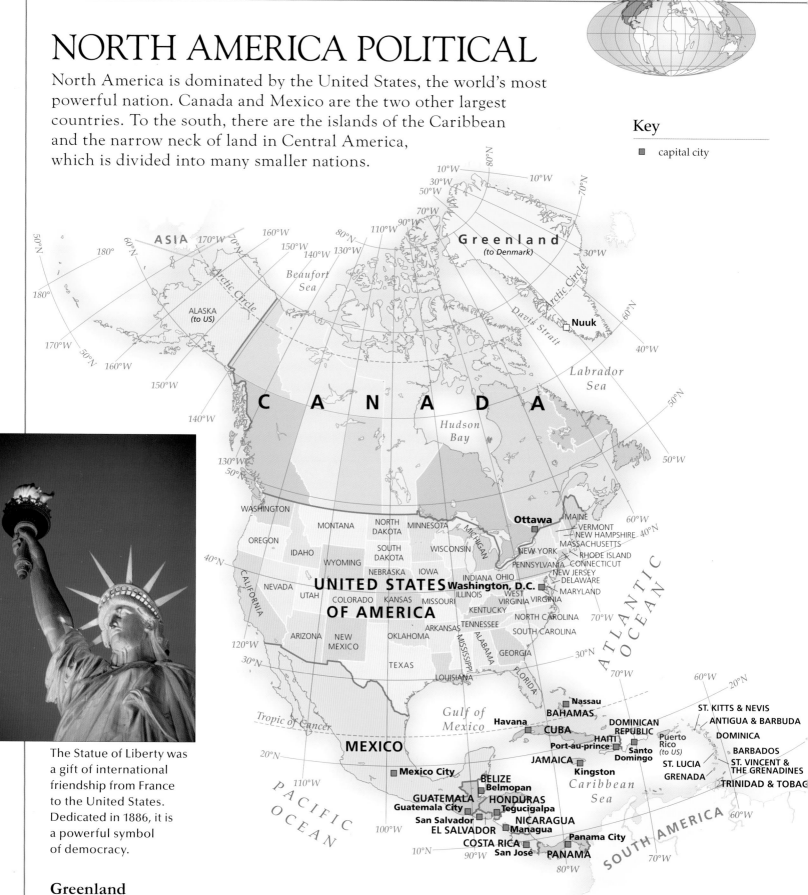

The Statue of Liberty was a gift of international friendship from France to the United States. Dedicated in 1886, it is a powerful symbol of democracy.

Greenland

Greenland, the world's largest island, lies on the eastern edge of North America. Most of the land is covered by a thick ice sheet that has been left over from the last Ice Age. Only around 50,000 people live in Greenland, the majority of whom are Inuit.

Scale 1:49,000,000

0   250   500   750   1,000 miles

NORTH AMERICA PHYSICAL

North America stretches from the Arctic to the Tropics. To the west, the Rockies form a high mountain chain and a barrier to climate and communications. To the east, the Great Plains are a vast area of flat land drained by the Mississippi River. The Great Lakes, on the border between the United States and Canada, are another key feature, created by glaciers in the last Ice Age.

NORTH AMERICA FACTS

HIGHEST MOUNTAIN: Mount McKinley 20,322 ft

LONGEST RIVER: Mississippi/Missouri 3,740 miles

BIGGEST LAKE: Lake Superior 31,820 sq miles

BIGGEST ISLAND: Greenland 836,330 sq miles

BIGGEST DESERT: Great Basin Desert 189,962 sq miles

BIGGEST COUNTRY: Canada 3,849,674 sq miles

SMALLEST COUNTRY: Saint Kitts & Nevis 104 sq miles

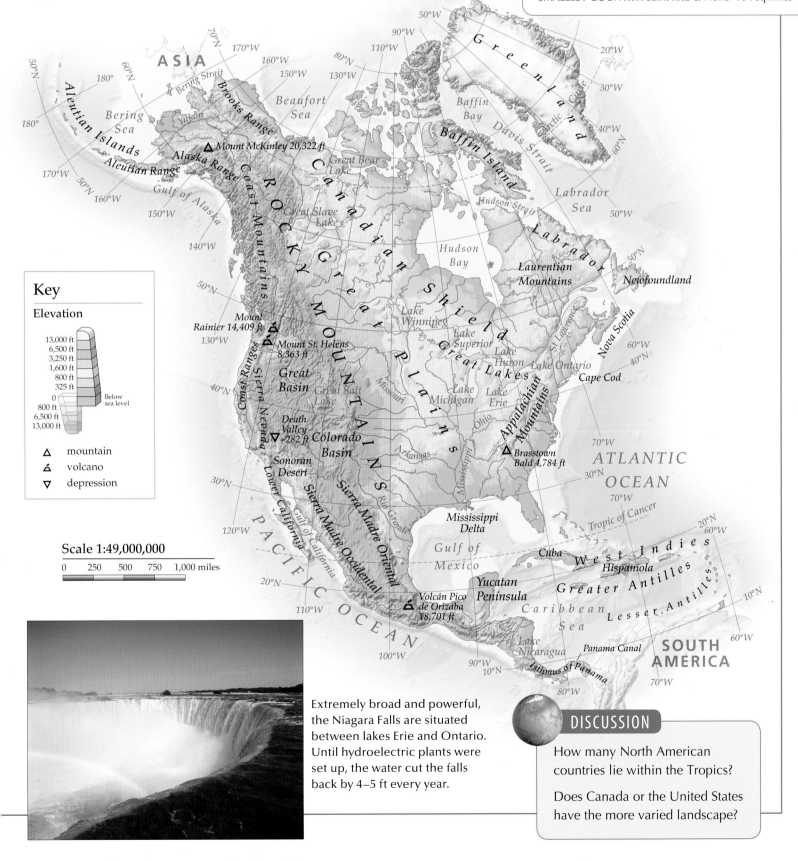

Key

Elevation

13,000 ft
6,500 ft
3,250 ft
1,600 ft
800 ft
325 ft
0
800 ft
6,500 ft
13,000 ft

Below sea level

△ mountain

⌃ volcano

▽ depression

Scale 1:49,000,000

0 250 500 750 1,000 miles

Extremely broad and powerful, the Niagara Falls are situated between lakes Erie and Ontario. Until hydroelectric plants were set up, the water cut the falls back by 4–5 ft every year.

DISCUSSION

How many North American countries lie within the Tropics?

Does Canada or the United States have the more varied landscape?

NORTH AMERICA POPULATION

North America has many great cities, especially along the east and west coasts of the United States. Mexico City, the capital of Mexico, is one of the largest cities in the world. By contrast, Canada has vast empty spaces with the main settlements close to the United States border.

Cities are expanding across the United States. A new type of settlement, called an "edge city," is appearing at highway intersections between major cities. Tyson's Corner near Washington, D.C. is a typical example, dominated by offices and shopping malls.

Issues for the future

• Many people in North America are immigrants from other parts of the world. From time to time there have been tensions between communities.

• There are controversial plans to build a 600-mile barrier on the US-Mexico border to prevent illegal immigration into the US.

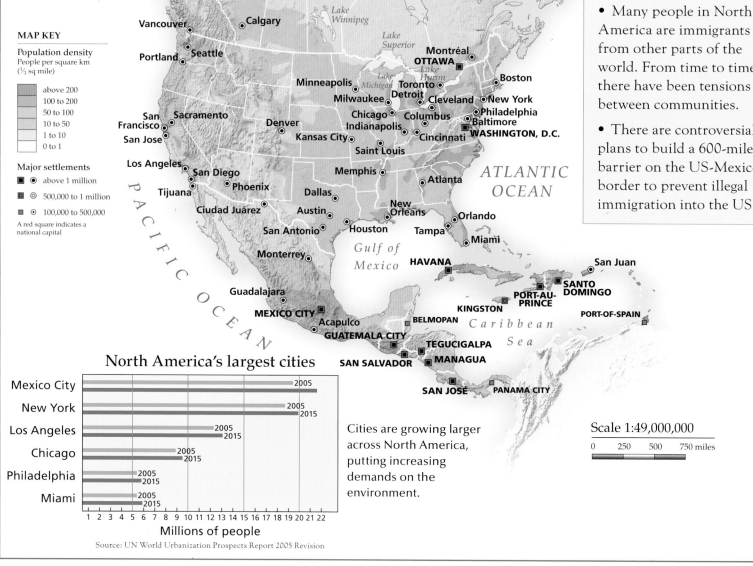

MAP KEY

Population density
People per square km
(⅓ sq mile)

	above 200
	100 to 200
	50 to 100
	10 to 50
	1 to 10
	0 to 1

Major settlements

■ ◉ above 1 million

▣ ◎ 500,000 to 1 million

▪ ⊙ 100,000 to 500,000

A red square indicates a national capital

Beaufort Sea
Baffin Bay
Bering Sea
Great Bear Lake
Great Slave Lake
Labrador Sea
Hudson Bay
Lake Winnipeg

Vancouver · Calgary
Portland · Seattle
Lake Superior
Montréal · **OTTAWA**
Lake Huron · Lake Michigan · Toronto · Boston
Minneapolis · Detroit · Cleveland · New York
Milwaukee · Chicago · Columbus · Philadelphia
San Francisco · Sacramento · Denver · Indianapolis · Baltimore
San Jose · Kansas City · Cincinnati · **WASHINGTON, D.C.**
Saint Louis
Los Angeles · San Diego · Memphis · Atlanta · *ATLANTIC OCEAN*
Tijuana · Phoenix · Dallas
Ciudad Juárez · Austin · New Orleans · Orlando
San Antonio · Houston · Tampa
Monterrey · Miami
Gulf of Mexico · **HAVANA** · San Juan
Guadalajara · **SANTO DOMINGO**
MEXICO CITY · **PORT-AU-PRINCE**
Acapulco · **KINGSTON** · **PORT-OF-SPAIN**
GUATEMALA CITY · **BELMOPAN** · *Caribbean Sea*
SAN SALVADOR · **TEGUCIGALPA**
MANAGUA
SAN JOSÉ · **PANAMA CITY**

PACIFIC OCEAN

North America's largest cities

Mexico City	2005	
New York	2005 / 2015	
Los Angeles	2005 / 2015	
Chicago	2005 / 2015	
Philadelphia	2005 / 2015	
Miami	2005 / 2015	

1 2 3 4 5 6 7 8 9 10 11 12 13 14 15 16 17 18 19 20 21 22
Millions of people

Source: UN World Urbanization Prospects Report 2005 Revision

Cities are growing larger across North America, putting increasing demands on the environment.

Scale 1:49,000,000

0   250   500   750 miles

NORTH AMERICA CLIMATE

The climate of North America varies from the intense cold of the polar regions to the hot and humid conditions found in the Caribbean. The Rocky Mountains are dry and arid, and there are deserts in the southwest of the United States and Mexico. Tornadoes and hurricanes affect some areas.

Scale 1:49,000,000

0   250   500   750 miles

MAP KEY

Climate regions

- polar
- tundra
- subarctic
- cool continental
- temperate
- warm temperate
- mediterranean
- semiarid
- arid
- tropical
- humid equatorial
- mountain

Map labels: Bering Sea, Brooks Range, Beaufort Sea, Baffin Bay, Greenland, Alaska Range, Great Bear Lake, Labrador Sea, Great Slave Lake, Canadian Shield, Hudson Bay, Laurentian Mountains, Rocky Mountains, Great Plains, Lake Winnipeg, Lake Superior, Lake Huron, Great Lakes, Lake Ontario, Lake Michigan, Lake Erie, Appalachian Mountains, ATLANTIC OCEAN, Great Basin, Sierra Nevada, Mojave Desert, Sonoran Desert, Sierra Madre Oriental, Sierra Madre Occidental, Gulf of Mexico, PACIFIC OCEAN, Sierra Madre del Sur, Caribbean Sea, Lake Nicaragua

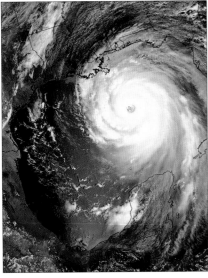

The structure of a hurricane is clearly visible from the air. Here, Hurricane Katrina is shown spiraling toward New Orleans in August 2005.

In polar regions, curtains of light caused by the earth's magnetic field sometimes flicker across the night sky. In North America, Europe, and Asia, they are known as aurora borealis, or northern lights. This photograph of the lights was taken in northern Canada.

Issues for the future

- Hurricanes and tornadoes are becoming more severe, perhaps as a result of global warming.

- Much of Mexico and the western US is extremely dry. Desert cities like Las Vegas put pressure on water resources.

NORTH AMERICA LAND USE

In the United States wheat and soybeans are important crops.
Some farmers keep animals on ranches. In the south and around
the Caribbean there are plantations of cotton, sugar cane,
coffee, and bananas. To the north, coniferous forests
spread across central Canada. There are great frozen
wastes in the polar regions, while other areas are
dominated by mountains and deserts.

Scale 1:46,000,000

| 0 | 250 | 500 | 750 | 1,000 miles |

MAP KEY

Landuse type

- polar
- tundra
- wetland
- forest
- pasture
- cropland
- desert
- mountain

industrial area

major conurbation

Issues for the future

- Soil erosion affects
many cropland areas.
In large parts of the US
soil is being lost faster
than it is forming.

- More than half the
world's genetically
modified crops are grown
in the US.

- In Greenland, glaciers
are retreating fast as the
climate changes.

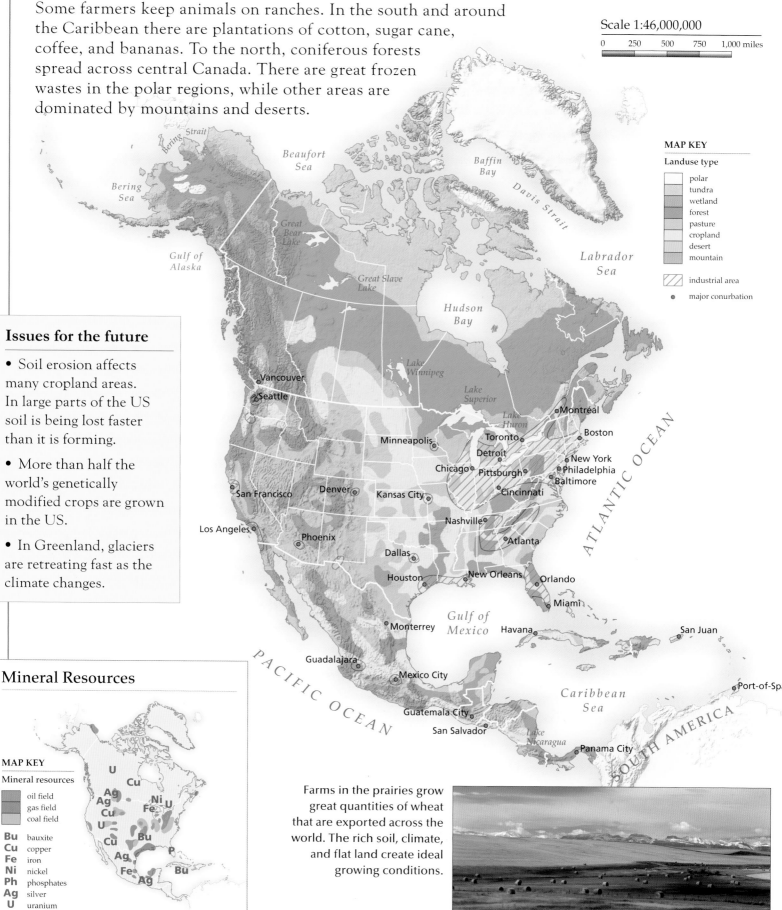

Mineral Resources

MAP KEY

Mineral resources

- oil field
- gas field
- coal field

Bu	bauxite
Cu	copper
Fe	iron
Ni	nickel
Ph	phosphates
Ag	silver
U	uranium

Farms in the prairies grow
great quantities of wheat
that are exported across the
world. The rich soil, climate,
and flat land create ideal
growing conditions.

NORTH AMERICA ENVIRONMENT

There are many natural wonders in North America. These include the Everglades marshes in Florida, the Grand Canyon on the Colorado River, and the great pillars of stone in Monument Valley, Arizona. However, the environment is under pressure from development and industrial pollution. As a result, some major natural habitats, such as the Arctic wilderness and the tropical rain forests, are under threat.

MAP KEY

Environmental issues

- existing forest
  existing desert
- desertification
  deforestation
- marine pollution
  heavy marine pollution
  acid rain

- polluted river
- poor urban air quality
- major oil spill
- nuclear test site
- nuclear accident

Issues for the future

- Acid rain is damaging lakes and forests in eastern Canada and the US.

- Nuclear accidents and oil spills have created serious problems in some areas.

- Climate change is threatening the balance of life in polar regions.

- Bush fires are an increasing environmental problem in Caifornia.

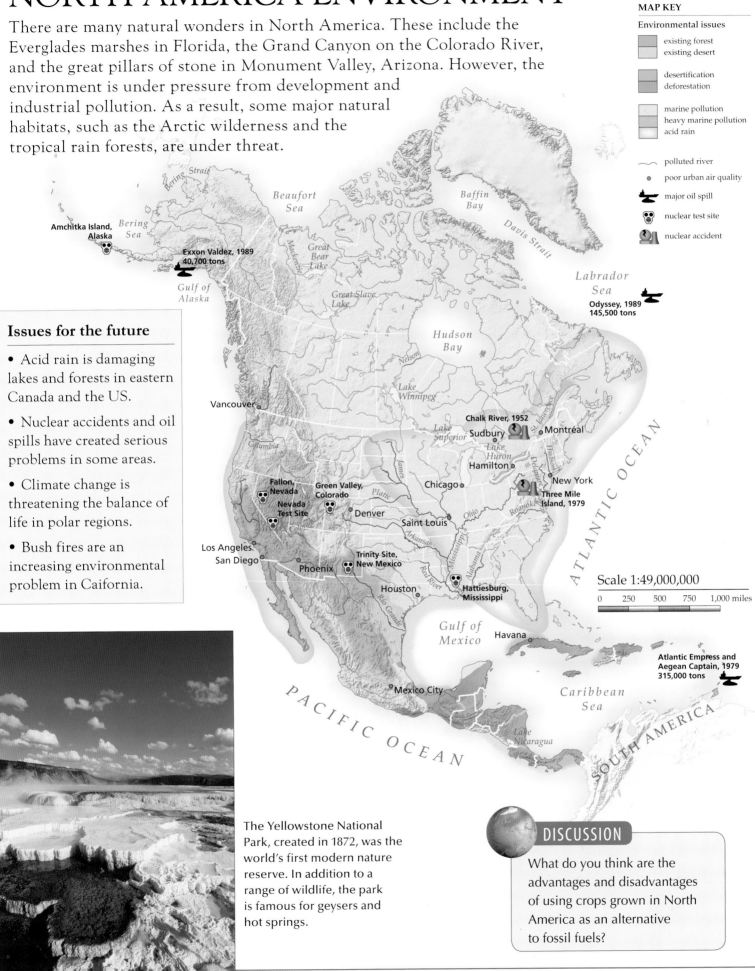

Amchitka Island, Alaska

Bering Strait · Bering Sea · Beaufort Sea · Baffin Bay · Davis Strait

Exxon Valdez, 1989
40,700 tons

Gulf of Alaska

Great Bear Lake · Great Slave Lake · Mackenzie · Nelson

Hudson Bay

Labrador Sea

Odyssey, 1989
145,500 tons

Vancouver

Lake Winnipeg

Chalk River, 1952

Lake Superior · Sudbury · Montréal

Lake Huron · Hamilton

Columbia · James

Fallon, Nevada · Green Valley, Colorado · Chicago · Platte

Nevada Test Site · Denver

Saint Louis

New York
Three Mile Island, 1979

Los Angeles
San Diego

Trinity Site, New Mexico

Phoenix

Houston

Hattiesburg, Mississippi

Colorado · Rio Grande · Red River · Arkansas · Mississippi · Alabama · Ohio

Gulf of Mexico   Havana

Mexico City

Caribbean Sea

Atlantic Empress and Aegean Captain, 1979
315,000 tons

ATLANTIC OCEAN

PACIFIC OCEAN

Lake Nicaragua

SOUTH AMERICA

Scale 1:49,000,000

0   250   500   750   1,000 miles

The Yellowstone National Park, created in 1872, was the world's first modern nature reserve. In addition to a range of wildlife, the park is famous for geysers and hot springs.

DISCUSSION

What do you think are the advantages and disadvantages of using crops grown in North America as an alternative to fossil fuels?

NORTH AMERICA FROM THE SKY

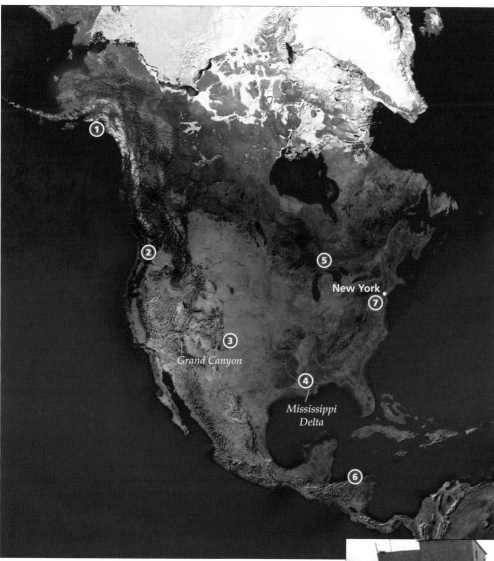

Environmental hot spots

1 Oil spill, Exxon Valdez, Alaska, 1989

2 Eruption, Mount St. Helens, US, 1980

3 Dust bowl disaster, US, 1930s

4 Hurricane Katrina, New Orleans, Louisiana, 2005

5 Acid rain, Great Lakes, ongoing

6 Hurricane Mitch, Nicaragua/Honduras, 1998

7 Nuclear accident, Three Mile Island, US, 1979

The arid areas in the southwest of the United States and Rocky Mountains are shown in brown in this satellite image. Farther north and east, the prairies give way to forests. The Arctic Ocean and Greenland are covered by ice.

Hurricane damage, Honduras

October 1998

More than 20,000 people died and 3 million people were affected when Hurricane Mitch struck Nicaragua and Honduras. Although there were ferocious winds, the rain caused even greater problems because the storm was unusually slow-moving.

US at night

This night image reveals the pattern of cities and settlements across the United States. Note how strings of lights along the highways link some of the main towns and cities.

New York City

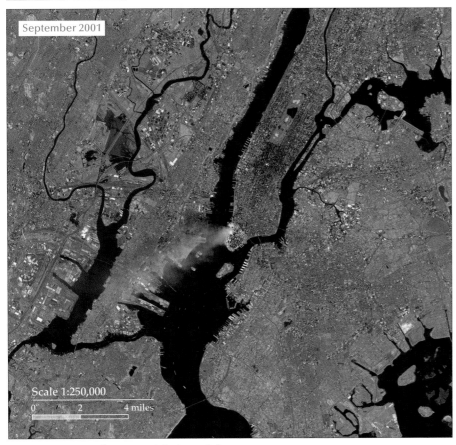

September 2001

Scale 1:250,000

0   2   4 miles

This image provides an aerial view of the buildings, waterways, and open space in New York. It was taken soon after the terrorist attacks on the Twin Towers. Smoke can be seen drifting from lower Manhattan.

Grand Canyon, Colorado River

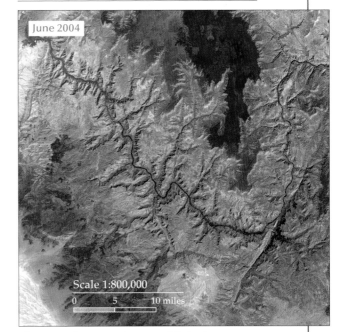

June 2004

Scale 1:800,000

0   5   10 miles

The Grand Canyon is a World Heritage Site famous for its landscape, geology, and wildlife. This infrared image was taken in early summer. Vegetation is shown in red, forests in brown, and bare rock in gray.

Mississippi Delta

Gulf of Mexico

May 2001

When the Mississippi River reaches the sea, strong currents cause sediments to create a "bird's foot" delta. The shape of the delta is constantly changing as new channels form and others become blocked. This causes problems for shipping.

Winter snowstorms

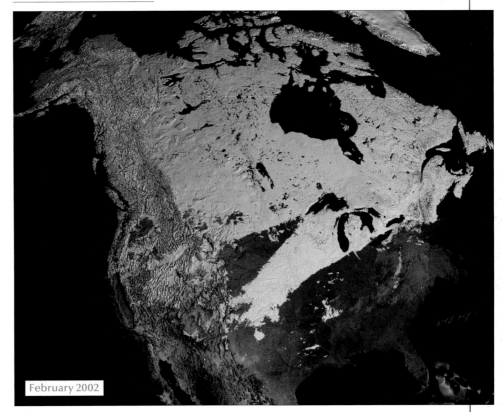

February 2002

This image shows the areas that have been hit by snowstorms. In the west of the United States, people depend on melting snow for most of their water. Satellites can help to monitor weather events.

CANADA AND GREENLAND

Canada is the world's second largest country and has by far the longest coastline. Most people live in the south near the border with the US. Here the climate is less severe than elsewhere. Farther north, huge expanses of coniferous forest dotted with lakes eventually lead to the frozen lands around the Arctic Ocean. The Rockies are a high mountain chain along the western seaboard.

This moraine lake in the Rocky Mountains, Alberta, is popular with hikers.

Key

Elevation

13,000 ft
6,500 ft
3,250 ft
1,600 ft
800 ft
325 ft
0
800 ft
6,500 ft
13,000 ft

Below sea level

△ mountain

Settlements

■ ⊙ over 1 million

◎ 500,000 to 1 million

⊙ 100,000 to 500,000

○ below 100,000

A red square indicates a national capital

ARCTIC OCEAN

Queen Elizabeth Islands

Axel Heiberg Island

Ellef Ringnes Island

Isachsen

Prince Patrick Island

Parry Islands

Mould Bay

Bathurst Island

Melville Island

Resolute

Viscount Melville Sound

Banks Island

Somerset Island

Prince of Wales Island

Beaufort Sea

Boothia Peninsula

Amundsen Gulf

Holman Victoria Island

McClintock Channel

Cambridge Bay

Inuvik

Kugluktuk

Arctic Circle

Fort Good Hope

NUNAVUT

ALASKA (part of US)

YUKON TERRITORY

Mackenzie Mountains

Great Bear Lake

Echo Bay

Bluenose

Back

Garry Lake

ROCKY

Mount Logan 19,551 ft

Gulf of Alaska

Whitehorse

Tungsten

NORTHWEST TERRITORIES

Yellowknife

Dubawnt Lake

Canada

Watson Lake

Great Slave Lake

Arviat

Fort Smith

Lake Athabasca

Churchill

PACIFIC OCEAN

BRITISH COLUMBIA

Williston Lake

Fort St John

CANADA

SASKATCHEWAN

Reindeer Lake

Fox Mine

Prince Rupert

Queen Charlotte Islands

Queen Charlotte Sound

Prince George

ALBERTA

Buffalo Narrows

MANITOBA

The Pas

Port Hardy

Mount Waddington 13,176 ft

Edmonton

Mount Robson 12,972 ft

North Saskatchewan

Leduc

Saskatchewan

Lake Winnipeg

Vancouver Island

Kamloops

Red Deer

Saskatoon

Victoria

Vancouver

Kelowna

Calgary

Regina

Lake Manitoba

Winnipeg

Lethbridge

Brandon

UNITED STATES OF AMERICA

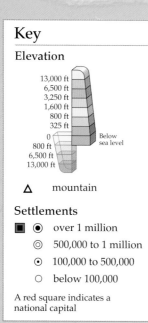

Greenland
(to Denmark)

Gunnbjørn Field
12,139 ft

Alert

Knud Rasmussen Land

Kong Frederik VIII Land

Kong Christian IX Land

Ammassalik

Nuuk

Qaqortoq

Baffin Bay

Davis Strait

Baffin Island

Lancaster Sound

Igloolik

Prince Charles Island

Nettilling Lake

Melville Peninsula

Foxe Basin

Repulse Bay

Amadjuak Lake

Hall Peninsula

Iqaluit

Cumberland Sound

Meta Incognita Peninsula

Resolution Island

Coral Harbour

Southampton Island

Hudson Strait

Akpatok Island

Ivujivik

Ungava Peninsula

Ungava Bay

Labrador Sea

Coats Island

Mansel Island

Ottawa Islands

Rankin Inlet

Inukjuak

Hudson Bay

A

Belcher Islands

Fort Severn

Caniapiscau

Nain

Cape Harrison

NEWFOUNDLAND & LABRADOR

St. Anthony

Réservoir de Caniapiscau

Smallwood Reservoir

Gander

QUÉBEC

James Bay

Akimiski Island

Labrador City

Newfoundland

St. Johns

Cape Race

Réservoir Manicouagan

Strait of Belle Isle

Gulf of St. Lawrence

Cabot Strait

St. Pierre and Miquelon
(to France)

Moosonee

Lac Mistassini

Baie-Comeau

Jonquière

Glace Bay

Cape Breton Island

ONTARIO

Cochrane

Charlesbourg

Fredericton

PRINCE EDWARD ISLAND

Charlottetown

Lake Nipigon

Trois-Rivières

Québec

St. John

Dartmouth

Halifax

Thunder Bay

Albany

Sherbrooke

NOVA SCOTIA

Sudbury

North Bay

Laval

Yarmouth

Bay of Fundy

Sault Ste.Marie

Georgian Bay

Montréal

Ottawa

NEW BRUNSWICK

Lake Superior

Peterborough

Lake Huron

Oshawa

Lake Michigan

Toronto

London

Lake Ontario

Niagara Falls

Windsor

Lake Erie

Laurentian Mountains

ATLANTIC OCEAN

The ice sheet that covers Greenland is more than 2 miles thick and contains 10 percent of the world's freshwater. If rising temperatures cause the ice to melt, sea levels will rise and there will be flooding worldwide.

WHAT ARE THE PRAIRIES?

The treeless plains of central US and southern Canada are known as the prairies. Here farms growing wheat and other crops stretch as far as the eye can see. Most of the grain is exported to other countries, which adds to North America's great political power.

Scale 1:20,000,000
(projection: Lambert Conformal Conic)

0   150   300   450   600 miles

1 inch on the map represents 316 miles on the ground

THE UNITED STATES OF AMERICA

The US is a federation of 50 states including Alaska and Hawaii. It is the wealthiest nation in the world, with great industrial cities on the seaboards and prosperous farmlands inland. Nearly half of the US is drained by the Mississippi River.

ALASKA

RUSSIAN FEDERATION

Prudhoe Bay
Beaufort Sea
Brooks Range
ALASKA (part of US)
Arctic Circle
CANADA
Wales
Yukon River
Fairbanks
Mount McKinley 20,322 ft
Alaska Range
Anchorage
Valdez
Platinum
Gulf of Alaska
Juneau

Bering Sea

Rat Islands
Atka
Aleutian Islands
Shumagin Islands
Alaska Peninsula
Kodiak Island
PACIFIC OCEAN

Scale 1:38,000,000
0   250   500 miles

The Grand Canyon in Arizona is one of the great natural wonders of the world. It has been created by the Colorado River, which has cut through the rocks to form a valley more than 1,900 ft deep.

Key

Elevation

13,000 ft
6,500 ft
3,250 ft
1,600 ft
800 ft
325 ft
0
800 ft — Below sea level
6,500 ft
13,000 ft

Settlements

⊙ over 1 million
◎ 500,000 to 1 million
⊙ 100,000 to 500,000
○ below 100,000

A red square indicates a national capital

△ mountain   ⌂ volcano

CANADA

Cape Flattery
Bellingham
Seattle WASHINGTON
Olympia
Spokane
Mount Rainier 14,409 ft
Mt. St. Helens 8,363 ft
Yakima
Columbia Basin
Havre
Portland
Columbia River
Salem
Eugene
Bend
OREGON
Harney Basin
Boise
IDAHO
Great Falls
MONTANA
Billings
Bitterroot Range
Missouri River
Crescent City
Yellowstone Lake
WYOMING
Coast Ranges
Cascade Ranges
UNITED
Casper
Sacramento Valley
Wells
Great Salt Lake
Rawlings
Reno
NEVADA
Salt Lake City
Santa Rosa
Sacramento
Great Salt Lake Desert
Provo
San Francisco
Oakland
Great Basin
UTAH
San Jose
Sierra Nevada
Salinas
San Joaquin Valley
Death Valley
Las Vegas
Cedar City
Lake Powell
Grand Canyon
Colorado Plateau
Bakersfield
Santa Barbara
Mojave Desert
Flagstaff
Santa Fe
Los Angeles
San Bernardino
ARIZONA
Albuquerque
NEW MEXICO
San Diego
Colorado River
Sonoran Desert
Phoenix
Tucson
Rio Grande
El Paso
MEXICO

PACIFIC OCEAN

HAWAI'I

Kaua'i
Ni'ihau
Līhu'e
O'ahu
Honolulu
Moloka'i
Wailuku
Maui
HAWAI'I (part of US)
Red Hill 10,023 ft
Mauna Kea 13,796 ft
Hilo
Hawai'i
Mauna Loa 13,678 ft

Scale 1:10,000,000
0   50   100 miles

A tornado snakes its way through rural Kansas after destroying a home. Kansas suffers more tornado damage than any other state in the US.

Map labels

CANADA

Lake of the Woods
Rainy Lake
Lake Superior
Great Lakes
Lake Huron
Lake Michigan
Lake Ontario
Lake Erie
Sault Sainte Marie
Niagara Falls

NORTH DAKOTA
Fargo
Bismarck
Badlands
Duluth
MINNESOTA
WISCONSIN
MICHIGAN
Green Bay
Lansing
Madison
Milwaukee
SOUTH DAKOTA
Rapid City
Sioux Falls
Minneapolis
Saint Paul
Chicago
Mississippi River
UNITED STATES

Cheyenne
NEBRASKA
Sioux City
Des Moines
Davenport
IOWA
INDIANA
OHIO
Omaha
North Platte River
Missouri River
Lincoln
Platte River
Denver
KANSAS
Kansas City
Springfield
ILLINOIS
Indianapolis
Colorado Springs
Topeka
Saint Louis
Louisville
Cincinnati
KENTUCKY
Lexington
AMERICA
Colorado
Wheeler Peak 13,160 ft
Dodge City
Wichita
MISSOURI
Springfield
Ozark Plateau
Nashville
Knoxville
Mount Mitchell △ 6,683 ft
Oklahoma City
Tulsa
ARKANSAS
Fort Smith
TENNESSEE
Memphis
Chattanooga
Canadian River
Amarillo
OKLAHOMA
Little Rock
Arkansas River
Mississippi River
Tennessee River
ALABAMA
Atlanta
Lubbock
Wichita Falls
Birmingham
GEORGIA
Carlsbad
Abilene
Dallas
Fort Worth
Shreveport
Jackson
Montgomery
Odessa
TEXAS
LOUISIANA
MISSISSIPPI
Mobile
Pecos River
Edwards Plateau
Colorado River
Beaumont
Baton Rouge
New Orleans
Pensacola
Tallahassee
FLORIDA
Austin
Lafayette
San Antonio
Houston
Galveston
Mississippi Delta
Gulf of Mexico
Orlando
Cape Canaveral
Tampa
Rio Grande
Victoria
Corpus Christi
Laredo
Padre Island
Brownsville
The Everglades
Florida Keys
Key West
Miami
Straits of Florida
BAHAMAS
CUBA
Tropic of Cancer

MAINE
NEW HAMPSHIRE
VERMONT
New England
Gulf of Maine
Saint John
Augusta
Portland
Montpelier
MASSACHUSETTS
Syracuse
Boston
Albany
Providence
Buffalo
NEW YORK
Hartford
RHODE ISLAND
CONNECTICUT
Newark
Long Island
New York
Detroit
PENNSYLVANIA
NEW JERSEY
Cleveland
Pittsburgh
Philadelphia
Columbus
Baltimore
DELAWARE
■ **Washington, D.C.**
WEST VIRGINIA
MARYLAND
VIRGINIA
Richmond
Charleston
Virginia Beach
Greensboro
NORTH CAROLINA
Cape Hatteras
Raleigh
Charlotte
Appalachian Mountains
Columbia
SOUTH CAROLINA
Cape Fear
Charleston
Savannah
St. Lawrence River
Hudson River
Ohio River
Jacksonville

ATLANTIC OCEAN

WHAT ARE TORNADOES?

Tornadoes are small but violent storms with a funnel that reaches from the base of the clouds to the ground below. These rotating winds can exceed 250 mph, causing terrible destruction. Tornadoes are found all over the world but they are particularly common in central US. It is thought they are caused by the mixing of cold and warm air in late spring and early summer.

Scale 1:13,000,000
(projection: Lambert Conformal Conic)

0   100   200   300   400 miles

1 inch on the map represents 205 miles on the ground

N W E S

A B 36 C D

CENTRAL AMERICA AND THE CARIBBEAN

A chain of high mountains, many of them volcanic, forms the spine of Central America. Mexico, with a population of over 100 million, is far larger than any of the other countries in the region. In the Caribbean, there are many small tropical islands that have become popular destinations for tourists from Europe and North America.

The Mayan civilization originated in the Yucatán Peninsula, Mexico. This photograph shows the Temple of Warriors in the ruined city of Chichen Itza. It was built AD 1100–1300 and is now an important tourist attraction.

Tijuana
Mexicali
Ensenada
San Luis
115°W
110°W
Nogales
105°W
Ciudad Juárez
30°N
UNITED STATES OF AMERICA
Isla Cedros
Hermosillo
Nuevo Casas Grandes
Villa Acuña
100°W
30°N
Guerrero Negro
Guaymas
Ciudad Obregón
Chihuahua
Piedras Negras
25°N
Navojoa
Delicias
Nueva Rosita
Isla Magdalena
Los Mochis
Hidalgo del Parral
Monclova
Nuevo Laredo
95°W
90°W
Tropic of Cancer
Isla Santa Margarita
Culiacán
Torreón
Reynosa
115°W
La Paz
Saltillo
Monterrey
Gulf of Mexico
Santa Genoveva 7,894 ft
Miraflores
Durango
Laguna Madre
San Lucas Cape
Mazatlán
MEXICO
Zacatecas
Ciudad Victoria
Islas Tres Marías
Tepic
San Luis Potosí
Tampico
20°N
Puerto Vallarta
León
Laguna de Tamiahua
Yucatán Channel
Guanajuato
Mérida
Cancún
Guadalajara
Irapuato
Querétaro
Tuxpán
Colima
Morelia
Valladolid
110°W
Manzanillo
Uruapan
Toluca
Mexico City
Popocatépetl 17,887 ft
Campeche
Yucatán Peninsula
Cuernavaca
Puebla
Veracruz
Carmen
Chetumal
Lázaro Cárdenas
Cuautla
Tehuacán
Coatzacoalcos
Villahermosa
BELIZE
Chilpancingo
Tuxtepec
Volcán El Chichónal 3,478 ft
Belize City
Acapulco
Oaxaca
Belmopan
Gulf
15°N
Pinotepa Nacional
Salina Cruz
Tuxtla
Comitán
Bay Islan
La Ceiba
105°W
Gulf of Tehuantepec
Volcán Tacaná 13,428 ft
San Pedro Sula
100°W
95°W
Tapachula
Sierra Madre
HONDURA
Guatemala City
Tegucigalpa
GUATEMALA
San Salvador
San Miguel
EL SALVADOR
León
Chinandega
Managua
10°N
Granada
Volcán Concepción 5,28
Liber
90°W
Puntarenas

PACIFIC OCEAN

Founded in 1325 at a height of over 6,500 ft, Mexico City has grown into a great metropolis. The Angel of Independence monument stands at the heart of the city.

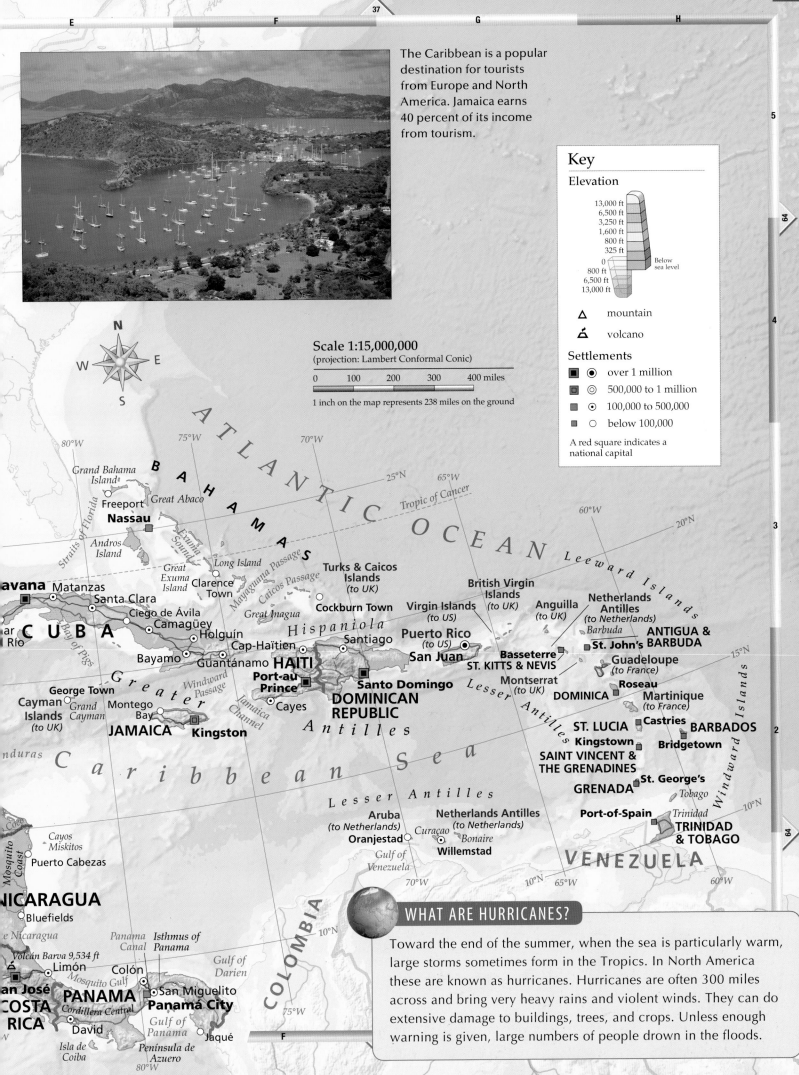

The Caribbean is a popular destination for tourists from Europe and North America. Jamaica earns 40 percent of its income from tourism.

Key

Elevation

13,000 ft
6,500 ft
3,250 ft
1,600 ft
800 ft
325 ft
0
800 ft
6,500 ft
13,000 ft

Below sea level

△ mountain

⌂ volcano

Settlements

■ ◉ over 1 million
◩ ◎ 500,000 to 1 million
▪ ◉ 100,000 to 500,000
▪ ○ below 100,000

A red square indicates a national capital

Scale 1:15,000,000
(projection: Lambert Conformal Conic)

0   100   200   300   400 miles

1 inch on the map represents 238 miles on the ground

N W E S

ATLANTIC OCEAN

80°W

B A H A M A S

Grand Bahama Island

Freeport
Nassau
Great Abaco

Straits of Florida

Andros Island

75°W

Great Exuma Island

Long Island

Clarence Town

Eleuthera Sound

Mayaguana Passage

Caicos Passage

70°W

25°N

Tropic of Cancer

65°W

Turks & Caicos Islands (to UK)

Cockburn Town

Great Inagua

60°W

20°N

Leeward Islands

British Virgin Islands (to UK)

Virgin Islands (to US)

Anguilla (to UK)

Netherlands Antilles (to Netherlands)

Barbuda

ANTIGUA & BARBUDA

St. John's

Havana
Matanzas
Santa Clara
Ciego de Ávila
Camagüey
Holguín
Bayamo
Guantánamo

Pinar del Rio

CUBA

Bay of Pigs

Cap-Haïtien
Santiago

Hispaniola

Puerto Rico (to US)

San Juan

Basseterre

ST. KITTS & NEVIS

Montserrat (to UK)

Guadeloupe (to France)

George Town
Cayman Islands (to UK)

Grand Cayman

Montego Bay

JAMAICA

Kingston

Greater

Windward Passage

Jamaica Channel

Cayes

HAITI

Port-au-Prince

Santo Domingo

DOMINICAN REPUBLIC

Lesser Antilles

DOMINICA

Roseau

Martinique (to France)

ST. LUCIA

Castries

BARBADOS

Bridgetown

Honduras

Caribbean Sea

Antilles

15°N

Kingstown

SAINT VINCENT & THE GRENADINES

GRENADA

St. George's

Windward Islands

Lesser Antilles

Tobago

Port-of-Spain

Trinidad

TRINIDAD & TOBAGO

Cayos Miskitos

Puerto Cabezas

Mosquito Coast

NICARAGUA

Bluefields

Lake Nicaragua

Aruba (to Netherlands)

Oranjestad

Curaçao

Bonaire

Netherlands Antilles (to Netherlands)

Willemstad

Gulf of Venezuela

70°W

10°N

VENEZUELA

65°W

60°W

10°N

COLOMBIA

Panama Canal

Isthmus of Panama

Gulf of Darien

Volcán Barva 9,534 ft

Limón

Colón

San Miguelito

PANAMA

Panamá City

San José

COSTA RICA

David

Cordillera Central

Gulf of Panama

Jaqué

Isla de Coiba

Península de Azuero

80°W

75°W

WHAT ARE HURRICANES?

Toward the end of the summer, when the sea is particularly warm, large storms sometimes form in the Tropics. In North America these are known as hurricanes. Hurricanes are often 300 miles across and bring very heavy rains and violent winds. They can do extensive damage to buildings, trees, and crops. Unless enough warning is given, large numbers of people drown in the floods.

SOUTH AMERICA POLITICAL

There are 12 independent countries in South America, plus French Guiana, which is governed by France. Brazil is by far the largest country, covering about half the continent and containing half of South America's population. Once a Portuguese colony, Brazil's official language is Portuguese. Elsewhere Spanish is the main language, again reflecting historical links.

The Falkland Islands (Islas Malvinas)

The Falkland Islands are 300 miles off the coast of Argentina. Originally uninhabited, they attracted settlers from France, Spain, Britain, and other countries. In 1982, a dispute between Argentina and the UK led to war. Both countries still claim ownership.

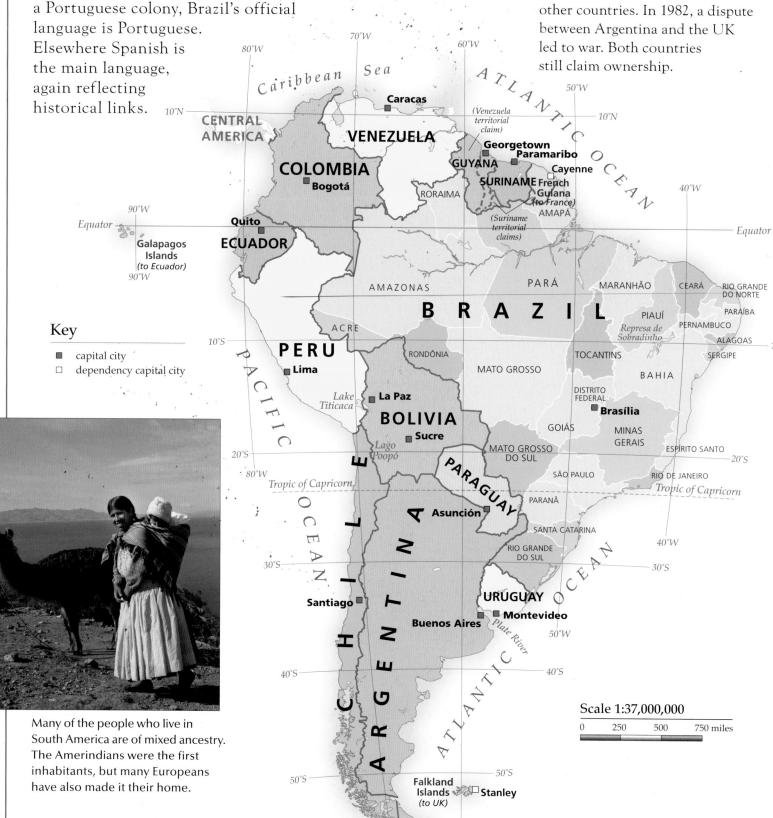

Key

■ capital city
□ dependency capital city

Scale 1:37,000,000

0   250   500   750 miles

Many of the people who live in South America are of mixed ancestry. The Amerindians were the first inhabitants, but many Europeans have also made it their home.

SOUTH AMERICA PHYSICAL

The longest mountain chain in the world, the Andes runs down the western edge of South America. From here, the Amazon flows eastward through rain forests and grasslands to the Atlantic Ocean. South America narrows as it approaches Antarctica. Cape Horn at the southern tip is famous for cold winds and turbulent waves.

SOUTH AMERICA FACTS

HIGHEST MOUNTAIN: Cerro Aconcagua 22,831 ft

LONGEST RIVER: Amazon 4,058 miles

BIGGEST LAKE: Lake Titicaca, Bolivia/Peru 3,300 sq miles

BIGGEST ISLAND: Tierra del Fuego 18,572 sq miles

BIGGEST DESERT: Patagonian Desert 100,387 sq miles

BIGGEST COUNTRY: Brazil 3,300,015 sq miles

SMALLEST COUNTRY: Suriname 63,039 sq miles

Scale 1:41,000,000

0   250   500   750 miles

Key

Elevation

13,000 ft
6,500 ft
3,250 ft
1,600 ft
800 ft
325 ft
0
800 ft   Below
6,500 ft   sea level
13,000 ft

△ mountain
⌂ volcano
▽ depression

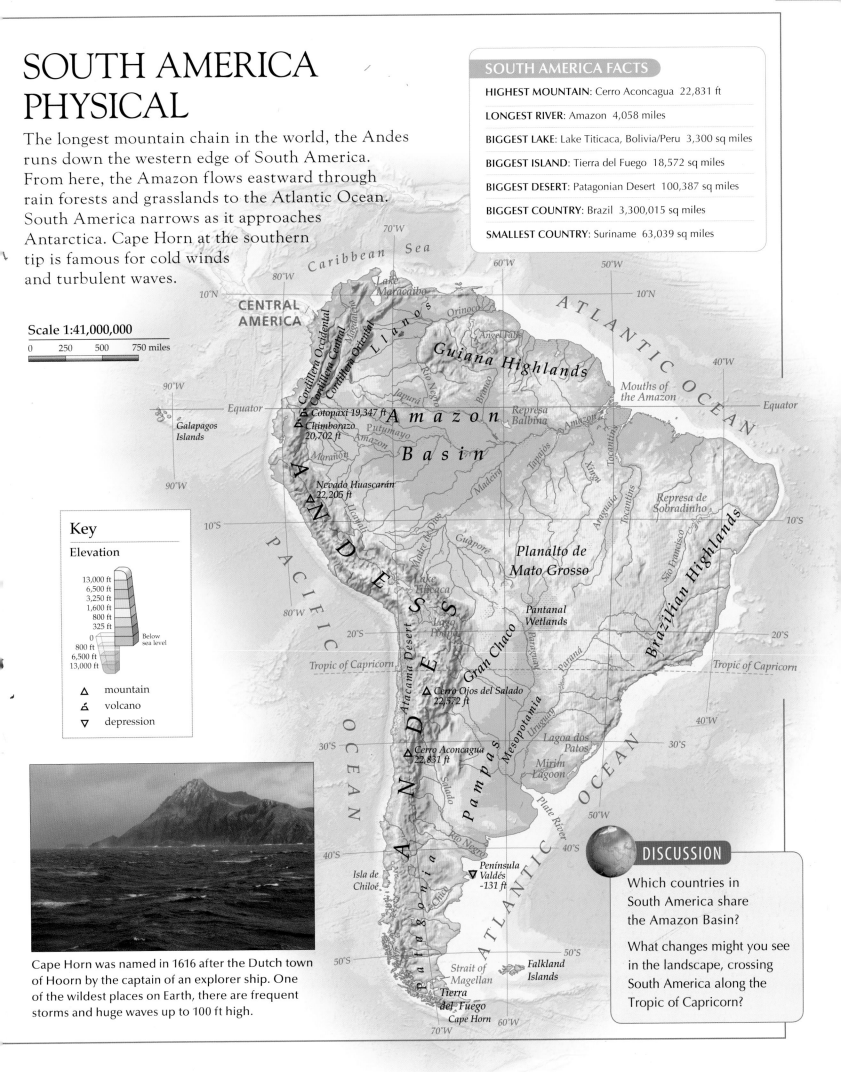

Cape Horn was named in 1616 after the Dutch town of Hoorn by the captain of an explorer ship. One of the wildest places on Earth, there are frequent storms and huge waves up to 100 ft high.

DISCUSSION

Which countries in South America share the Amazon Basin?

What changes might you see in the landscape, crossing South America along the Tropic of Capricorn?

SOUTH AMERICA POPULATION

The population of South America is distributed very unevenly. Along the coast and in the mountains of the north many people live crowded together in cities. Inland there are vast empty areas. In the Amazon Basin new settlements are growing up as the forest is cleared for farmland.

South America's largest cities

Sao Paulo	2005 / 2015
Buenos Aires	2005 / 2015
Rio de Janeiro	2005 / 2015
Lima	2005 / 2015
Bogota	2005 / 2015
Santiago	2005 / 2015

1 2 3 4 5 6 7 8 9 10 11 12 13 14 15 16 17 18 19 20 21 22
Millions of people

Source: UN World Urbanization Prospects Report 2005 Revision

In South America, more people live in cities than on any other continent.

Issues for the future

• Many cities have grown very fast and are now surrounded by poor people living in shanties (makeshift dwellings).

• Water supply and waste disposal is a problem in many cities, along with air pollution.

• There are great differences in wealth between different regions.

La Paz, the capital of Bolivia, is the highest capital city in the world. It was founded by the Spanish in the 16th century on the site of a Native-American settlement.

Map labels

Caribbean Sea

ATLANTIC OCEAN

PACIFIC OCEAN

ATLANTIC OCEAN

Barranquilla, Cartagena, Maracaibo, CARACAS, Valencia, Maracay, Cumaná, San Cristóbal, Bucaramanga, Medellín, GEORGETOWN, PARAMARIBO, CAYENNE, BOGOTÁ, Cali, Pasto, Boa Vista, Esmeraldas, QUITO, Guayaquil, Iquitos, Manaus, Santarém, Belém, São Luís, Piura, Fortaleza, Natal, Trujillo, Porto Velho, Recife, Maceió, Palmas, Aracaju, Callao, LIMA, Cusco, Salvador, Arequipa, LA PAZ, Oruro, Santa Cruz, Cuiabá, BRASÍLIA, Arica, SUCRE, Goiânia, Antofagasta, Campo Grande, Belo Horizonte, Vitória, Salta, ASUNCIÓN, Campinas, Rio de Janeiro, São Paulo, Curitiba, Córdoba, Corrientes, Florianópolis, Coquimbo, Porto Alegre, Mendoza, Paraná, Rosario, SANTIAGO, BUENOS AIRES, MONTEVIDEO, La Plata, Plate River, Concepción, Mar del Plata, Bahía Blanca, Punta Arenas

Scale 1:33,500,000

0   250   500   750 miles

MAP KEY

Population density
People per square km
(⅓ sq mile)

	above 200
	100 to 200
	50 to 100
	10 to 50
	1 to 10

Major settlements

■ ● above 1 million

▣ ◉ 500,000 to 1 million

▪ ◎ 100,000 to 500,000

A red square indicates a national capital

SOUTH AMERICA CLIMATE

South America lies across the equator and much of the continent has a hot, wet climate. The Amazon Basin is one of the largest rain forest areas in the world. Farther south, conditions become more temperate and there are extensive grasslands. Deserts are found along the Pacific coast as well as in southern Argentina.

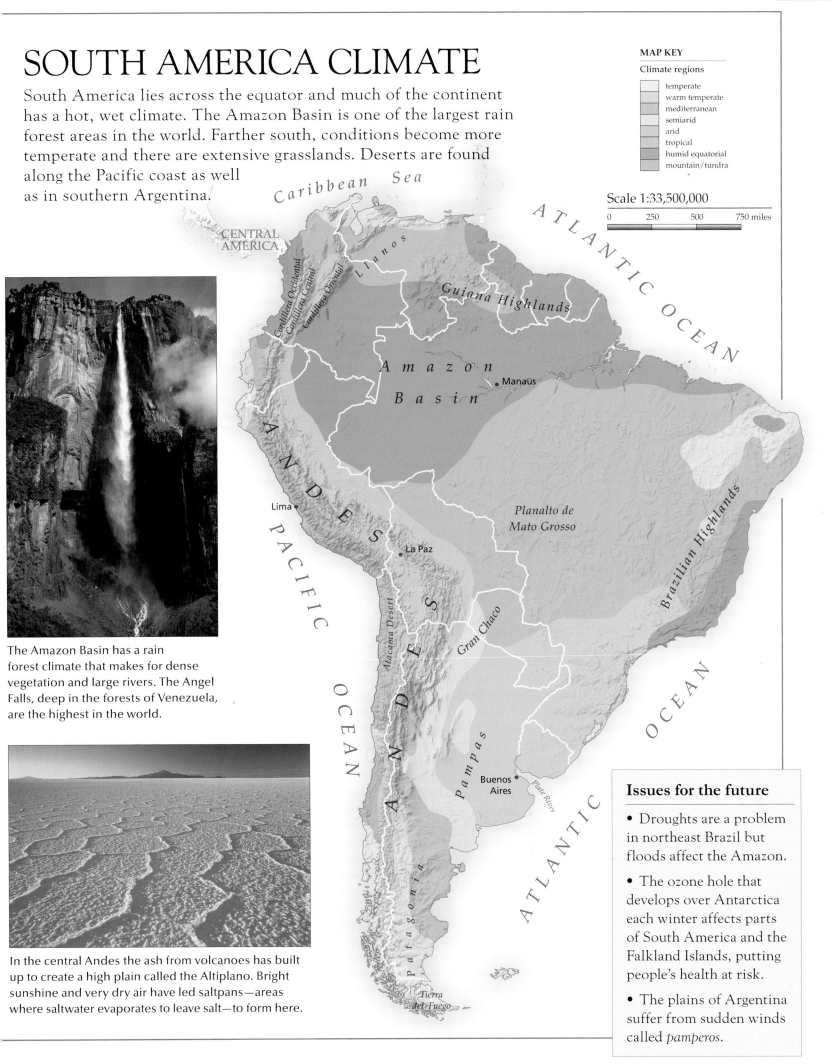

MAP KEY

Climate regions

- temperate
- warm temperate
- mediterranean
- semiarid
- arid
- tropical
- humid equatorial
- mountain/tundra

Scale 1:33,500,000

0   250   500   750 miles

The Amazon Basin has a rain forest climate that makes for dense vegetation and large rivers. The Angel Falls, deep in the forests of Venezuela, are the highest in the world.

In the central Andes the ash from volcanoes has built up to create a high plain called the Altiplano. Bright sunshine and very dry air have led saltpans—areas where saltwater evaporates to leave salt—to form here.

Issues for the future

- Droughts are a problem in northeast Brazil but floods affect the Amazon.

- The ozone hole that develops over Antarctica each winter affects parts of South America and the Falkland Islands, putting people's health at risk.

- The plains of Argentina suffer from sudden winds called *pamperos*.

SOUTH AMERICA LAND USE

Large areas of Brazil, Peru, and Venezuela are covered by rain forest. Elsewhere, tropical crops, such as cotton, sugar cane, bananas, citrus fruit, and coffee, are grown on plantations, especially near the Atlantic coast. Cattle farming is one of the main activities in southern Brazil, Paraguay, and Argentina, along with growing cereals. There are important industrial areas around the cities.

Chile produces nearly a third of the world's copper. The mines are in the north of the country, in the Atacama desert. This photograph shows the Chuquicamata mine, a huge strip mine.

Issues for the future

• South American food is often sold cheaply to other countries, but prices are improving with fair trade deals.

• Brazil leads the world in using ethanol, a fuel made from sugar cane, as an ecofriendly source of fuel.

• Illegal drug users all over the world depend on cocaine grown in the Andes.

Mineral Resources

MAP KEY

Mineral resources

	oil field
	gas field
	coal field

Bu bauxite
Cu copper
Fe iron
Pb lead
Ag silver
Sn tin

Caribbean Sea

CENTRAL AMERICA

Barranquilla
Maracaibo
Caracas
Medellín
Bogotá
Cali
Guayaquil
Belém
Fortaleza
Manaus
Recife
Lima
Salvador
Brasília
Belo Horizonte
Rio de Janeiro
São Paulo
Curitiba
Porto Alegre
Córdoba
Rosario
Montevideo
Santiago
Buenos Aires

ATLANTIC OCEAN

PACIFIC OCEAN

ATLANTIC OCEAN

Plate River

Scale 1:33,500,000

| 0 | 250 | 500 | 750 miles |

MAP KEY

Land use type

	forest
	pasture
	cropland
	desert
	barren land
	mountain

industrial area

• major conurbation

SOUTH AMERICA ENVIRONMENT

South America has many natural wonders, from the towering peaks of the Andes to the Iguacu Falls in southern Brazil. One of the biggest challenges is to protect the Amazon Rain Forest from destruction. This is one of the world's richest ecosystems with a unique range of plants and creatures. The rain forest also has a significant impact on world climate patterns.

Issues for the future

• There are large numbers of volcanoes bringing danger from eruptions, earthquakes, and mudslides.

• Illegal trade in wildlife threatens endangered species in Brazil.

• The by-products of mining have polluted rivers and land in some areas, especially Brazil and Venezuela.

MAP KEY

Environmental issues

existing forest
existing desert

desertification
deforestation
marine pollution
heavy marine pollution

~~ polluted river
• poor urban air quality

Scale 1:37,000,000

0   250   500   750 miles

The Amazon Rain Forest is being cleared for cattle ranching and crops at an alarming rate. Fires started in the dry season burn the trees. An area the size of California was destroyed between 2000 and 2006. At this pace only a few areas will be left by 2050.

DISCUSSION

What do you think might be the best way of protecting the Amazon Rain Forest from destruction?

SOUTH AMERICA FROM THE SKY

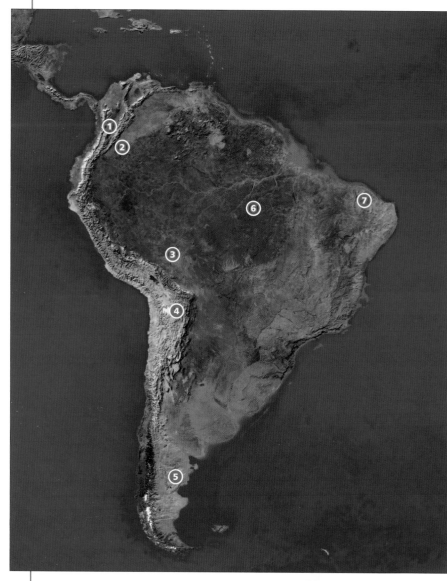

Environmental hot spots

1 Mudslide, Nevado del Ruiz, Colombia, 1984

2 Deforestation and soil loss, cocaine farming, Colombia, ongoing

3 Forest fires, Amazon rain forest, ongoing

4 Air, water, and land pollution, Cerro Rico mine, Bolivia, ongoing

5 Ozone hole, Patagonia, Argentina, 1980s onward

6 Illegal logging, Amazon, ongoing

7 Drought, northeast Brazil, ongoing

In this image, the Amazon Basin is shown in dark green and the Andes in brown. Notice how some of the peaks are capped with snow, especially toward Antarctica.

South America at night

Cerro Rico mine, Bolivia

c. 1995

The Cerro Rico mines have been producing silver and tin for hundreds of years, but now the minerals have been almost exhausted. Metal pollution now contaminates the soil and river water in the surrounding area.

The pattern of light blue dots shows the main cities in Brazil, Argentina, and the northwest. The coastline and country boundaries have been picked out in red in this image.

Brasilia

Glaciers, Argentina

1995

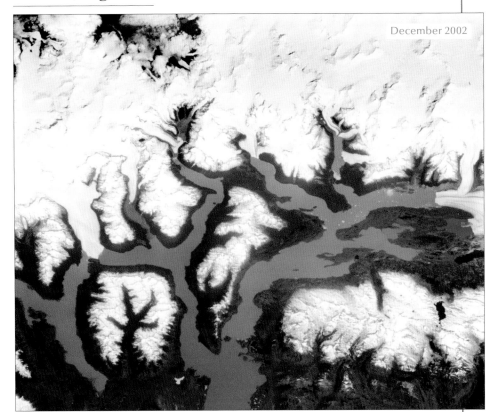

December 2002

Brasilia was created as the brand new capital of Brazil in 1960. In this false color image the buildings and streets are light blue, woods are brown, and lakes deep blue. As Brasilia grows larger, the buildings are extending farther and farther into the countryside.

These glaciers form part of an ice field in southern Argentina. As the ice melts, the water flows into a lake. The melt water, which is heavy in sediments, shows up in light blue in this photograph. The glaciers in this region are now retreating steadily, probably due to global warming.

Clearing the rain forest

September 2002

BRAZIL

Iguaçu River

ARGENTINA

The impact of human activity is shown very clearly in this photograph. To the south of the Iguaçu River, land has been cleared for agriculture. To the north, the rain forest remains untouched. People have different opinions about the benefits of these changes.

SOUTH AMERICA

Most of South America lies to the south of the equator. It contains the world's greatest rain forest, Amazonia, and the world's longest mountain range, the Andes. There are many active volcanoes here that have built up over millions of years.

Santiago, like many cities, is situated in a valley and suffers from pollution as fumes from cars and factories become trapped. The pure air and snow of the Andes can be seen above the haze.

ATLANTIC OCEAN

PACIFIC OCEAN

Caribbean Sea

Gulf of Venezuela

PANAMA

COLOMBIA

VENEZUELA

GUYANA

SURINAME

French Guiana (to France)

BRAZIL

Amazon Basin

Guiana Highlands

ECUADOR

PERU

ANDES

Bogotá

Caracas

Georgetown

Paramaribo

Cayenne

Kourou

Quito

Lima

Guayaquil

Barranquilla

Cartagena

Medellín

Cali

Bucaramanga

Cúcuta

Maracaibo

Barquisimeto

Valencia

Barinas

Riohacha

Montería

Pasto

Tumaco

Esmeraldas

Portoviejo

Machala

Cuenca

Loja

Piura

Punta Negra

Chimbote

Trujillo

Cajamarca

Huánuco

Pucallpa

Iquitos

Leticia

Mitú

Florencia

Tunja

Ciudad Bolívar

Angel Falls

Mount Roraima 9,219 ft

Pico da Neblina 9,889 ft

Boa Vista

Caracaraí

Manaus

Santarém

Belém

São Luís

Fortaleza

Natal

Recife

Maceió

Campina Grande

Teresina

Picos

Parnaíba

Mossoró

João Pessoa

Aracaju

Feira de Santana

Salvador

Floriano

Imperatriz

Bacabal

Marabá

Altamira

Macapá

Porto Velho

Ariquemes

Rio Branco

Riberalta

Barreiras

Paulas do Tocantins

TRINIDAD & TOBAGO

Isla de Margarita

Punta Gallinas

Lake Maracaibo

Rio Orinoco

Rio Negro

Amazon

Mouths of the Amazon

Ilha de Marajó

Represa Balbina

Represa de Tucuruí

Rio Tocantins

Rio São Francisco

Represa de Sobradinho

Rio Xingu

Serra dos Gradas

Serra Formosa

Rio São Manuel

Rio Tapajós

Rio Madeira

Rio Purus

Rio Juruá

Rio Japurá

Rio Putumayo

Rio Caquetá

Rio Napo

Rio Marañón

Rio Ucayali

Rio Juruena

Rio Guaporé

Chapada dos

Chapada Diamantina

Cabo de São Roque

Equator

Cusco

Ayacucho

Callao

Cabo de São Roque

The ruined city of Machu Picchu, high in the Andes of Peru, was built by the Incas in the 15th century and is now a major tourist attraction.

HOW WERE THE ANDES FORMED?

As the floor of the Pacific Ocean moves eastward under South America, it falls back into the interior of the earth. The rocks become hotter, any water turns to steam, and volcanoes break out on the surface. Over millions of years this has created a great mountain range.

Key

Elevation

- 13,000 ft
- 6,500 ft
- 3,250 ft
- 1,600 ft
- 800 ft
- 325 ft
- 0
- 800 ft
- 6,500 ft
- 13,000 ft
- Below sea level

△ mountain
⌁ volcano

Settlements

- ⊙ over 1 million
- ◎ 500,000 to 1 million
- ⊙ 100,000 to 500,000
- ○ below 100,000

■ A red square indicates a national capital

Scale 1:21,700,000
(projection: Lambert Azimuthal Equal Area)

0 150 300 450 600 miles

1 inch on the map represents 343 miles on the ground

PACIFIC OCEAN

ATLANTIC OCEAN

BRAZIL

Brazilian Highlands

BOLIVIA

PARAGUAY

URUGUAY

ARGENTINA

CHILE

Patagonia

Atacama Desert

Pampas

Gran Chaco

Pantanal

Falkland Islands (to UK)

West Falkland

East Falkland

Tierra del Fuego

Cape Horn

Drake Passage

Strait of Magellan

Beagle Channel

Isla de los Estados

Archipiélago de los Chonos

Isla de Chiloé

Gulf of San Jorge

Gulf of San Matías

Bahía Grande

Bahía Blanca

Mar del Plata

Plate River

Lagoa dos Patos

Lagoa Mirim

Mirim Lagoon

Iguazú Falls

Cordillera Occidental

Tropic of Capricorn

Cities and towns

Arequipa
Montes Claros
Governador Valadares
Belo Horizonte
Juiz de Fora
Vitória
Uberaba
Uberlândia
Goiânia
Campo Grande
Marília
Campinas
São Paulo
Nova Iguaçu
Rio de Janeiro
Santos
Curitiba
Florianópolis
Maringá
Passo Fundo
Canoas
Porto Alegre
Pedro Juan Caballero
Asunción
Ciudad del Este
Posadas
Santa Maria
Rio Grande
Bagé
Montevideo
Formosa
Resistencia
Concordia
Paraná
Mar del Plata
Necochea
Bahía Blanca
Tres Arroyos
Santa Rosa
Buenos Aires
Rosario
Córdoba
Santiago del Estero
La Rioja
Mendoza
San Juan
San Rafael
Neuquén
Coihaique
Puerto Montt
Concepción
Talca
Santiago
Viña del Mar
Coquimbo
Copiapó
Antofagasta
Calama
Iquique
Arica
Salta
San Miguel de Tucumán
Potosí
Oruro
Tarija
Sucre
La Paz
Santa Cruz
Rawson
Comodoro Rivadavia
Puerto San Julián
Punta Arenas
Stanley

Peaks

Nevado Sajama 21,391 ft
Volcán Misti 19,101 ft
Nevado de Chani 20,341 ft
Cerro Galán 21,654 ft
Cerro Ojos del Salado 22,572 ft
Cerro Aconcagua 22,831 ft
Cerro Paine 8,760 ft
Cerro San Valentin 13,314 ft

Rivers

Pilcomayo
Paraguay
Paraná
Uruguay
Bermejo

EUROPE POLITICAL

Although Europe is one of the smallest continents, it is divided into over 40 countries and contains more than 700 million people. Many new countries were created with the breakup of the Soviet Union (1989–1991). Other new countries were formed in southern Europe between 1991 and 2001 with the collapse of Yugoslavia.

Key

■ capital city

Scale 1:25,700,000

0   150   300   450 miles

Growth of the European Union

Founder members 1957
1. Netherlands
2. Belgium
3. Luxembourg
4. France
5. Germany
6. Italy

Joined 1973
7. Ireland
8. United Kingdom
9. Denmark

Joined 1981
10. Greece

Joined 1986
11. Portugal
12. Spain

Joined 1995
13. Sweden
14. Finland
15. Austria

Joined 2004
16. Estonia
17. Latvia
18. Lithuania
19. Poland
20. Czech Republic
21. Slovakia
22. Slovenia
23. Hungary
24. Cyprus
25. Malta

Joined 2007
26. Romania
27. Bulgaria

Possible new members
28. Croatia
29. Macedonia
30. Turkey

The European Union

Much of Europe lay in ruins after World War II (1939–1945) and had to be rebuilt. The leaders in France and Germany decided to work together to improve conditions and keep the peace. This was the start of the European Union. Since then the EU has grown to include 27 countries with a total population of 490 million people.

EUROPE PHYSICAL

Europe is about 2,486 miles across from north to south.
In the west it faces the Atlantic Ocean. In the east the Ural
Mountains form the border with Asia. The Alps are the
most important mountain range as well as being the source
of the Rhine River, which flows into the North Sea.

EUROPE FACTS

HIGHEST MOUNTAIN: Mount Elbrus 18,510 ft

LONGEST RIVER: Volga River 2,194 miles

BIGGEST LAKE: Lake Ladoga 6,834 sq miles

BIGGEST ISLAND: Great Britain 84,400 sq miles

BIGGEST DESERT: There are no deserts in Europe

BIGGEST COUNTRY: European Russia 1,658,077 sq miles

SMALLEST COUNTRY: Vatican City 0.17 sq miles

Key

Elevation

13,000 ft
6,500 ft
3,250 ft
1,600 ft
800 ft
325 ft
0
800 ft
6,500 ft
13,000 ft

Below
sea level

△ mountain
⌁ volcano
▽ depression

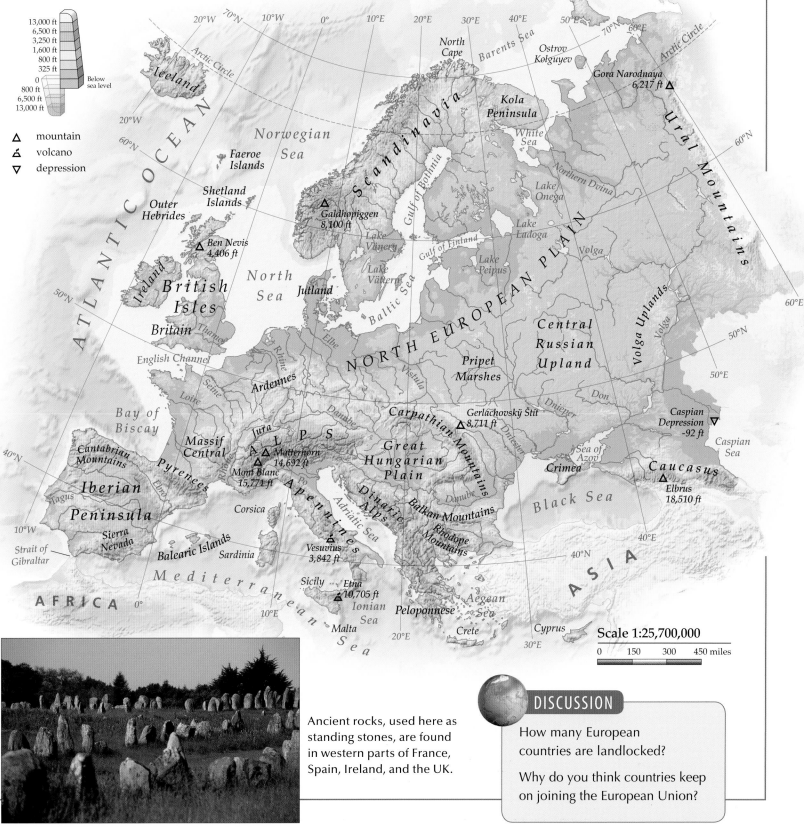

Scale 1:25,700,000

0   150   300   450 miles

Ancient rocks, used here as
standing stones, are found
in western parts of France,
Spain, Ireland, and the UK.

DISCUSSION

How many European
countries are landlocked?

Why do you think countries keep
on joining the European Union?

EUROPE FROM THE SKY

Carlisle

Amsterdam

Mount Etna

Environmental hot spots

1 Prestige oil spill, Atlantic Ocean, 2002

2 Forest fires, Portugal, 2005

3 Torrey Canyon oil spill, Scilly Isles, 1967

4 Avalanches, Austria, 2002

5 Acid rain damage, Czech Republic, 1970s onward

6 Nuclear submarine dumping, Barents Sea, 1950s onward

7 Nuclear accident, Chernobyl, Ukraine, 1986

The colors in this satellite image indicate different types of vegetation and land use. Arid areas in Spain, Turkey, and Ukraine are picked out in brown and yellow. Green represents woods and grassland. The Vatnajokull ice sheet in Iceland is light blue.

Prestige oil spill

November 2002

Seventy thousand tons of oil leaked from the wreck of the Prestige in 2002, killing wildlife and polluting beaches in Spain, Portugal, and France.

Europe at night

Towns and cities show up clearly on this nighttime image. London, Paris, Moscow, and Madrid appear as a blaze of light. The flares from oil rigs can be seen in the North Sea.

Flooding in Carlisle

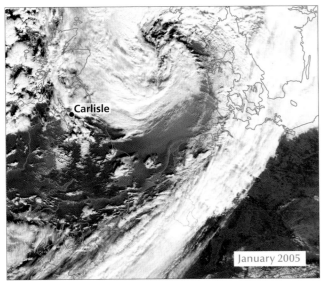

The Atlantic depression that swept across Britain and northwest Europe in January 2005 caused the worst flooding for a century in Carlisle and other parts of Cumbria, UK. The spiral of clouds in this photograph shows the position of weather fronts.

Mount Etna eruption

When Mount Etna erupted, the wind carried a plume of smoke and ash hundreds of miles across the eastern Mediterranean.

Amsterdam city center

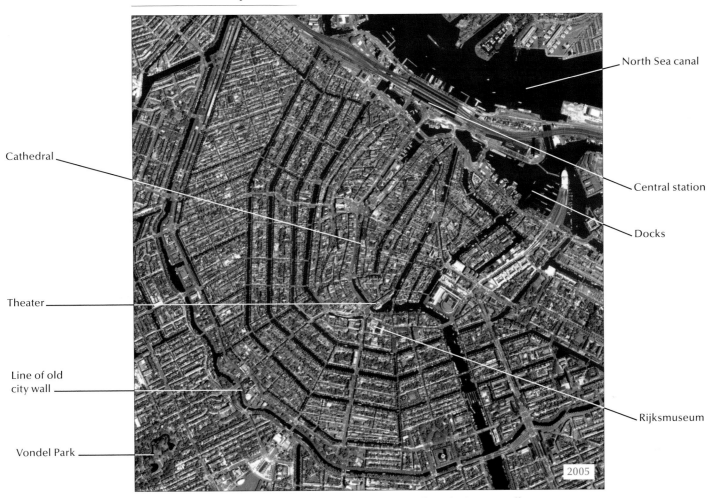

Founded in the 13th century, Amsterdam has grown from being a small port to a modern capital city. The pattern of streets and canals around the historic core, along with individual buildings, shows up clearly from the air.

NORTHERN EUROPE

Northern Europe is the coldest and emptiest part of the continent. There are icy mountains and deep fjords along the coast of Norway. Sweden and Finland are much flatter with many forests and lakes. The Baltic States (Estonia, Latvia, and Lithuania) have more land used for growing crops.

In Iceland there is intense volcanic activity. The Strokkur geyser, near Reykjavik, erupts every five to 10 minutes with water spouts up to 65 ft high.

Key

Elevation

13,000 ft
6,500 ft
3,250 ft
1,600 ft
800 ft
325 ft
0
800 ft
6,500 ft
13,000 ft
Below sea level

△ mountain
♨ volcano

Settlements

⊙ over 1 million
◎ 500,000 to 1 million
⊙ 100,000 to 500,000
○ below 100,000

A red square indicates a national capital

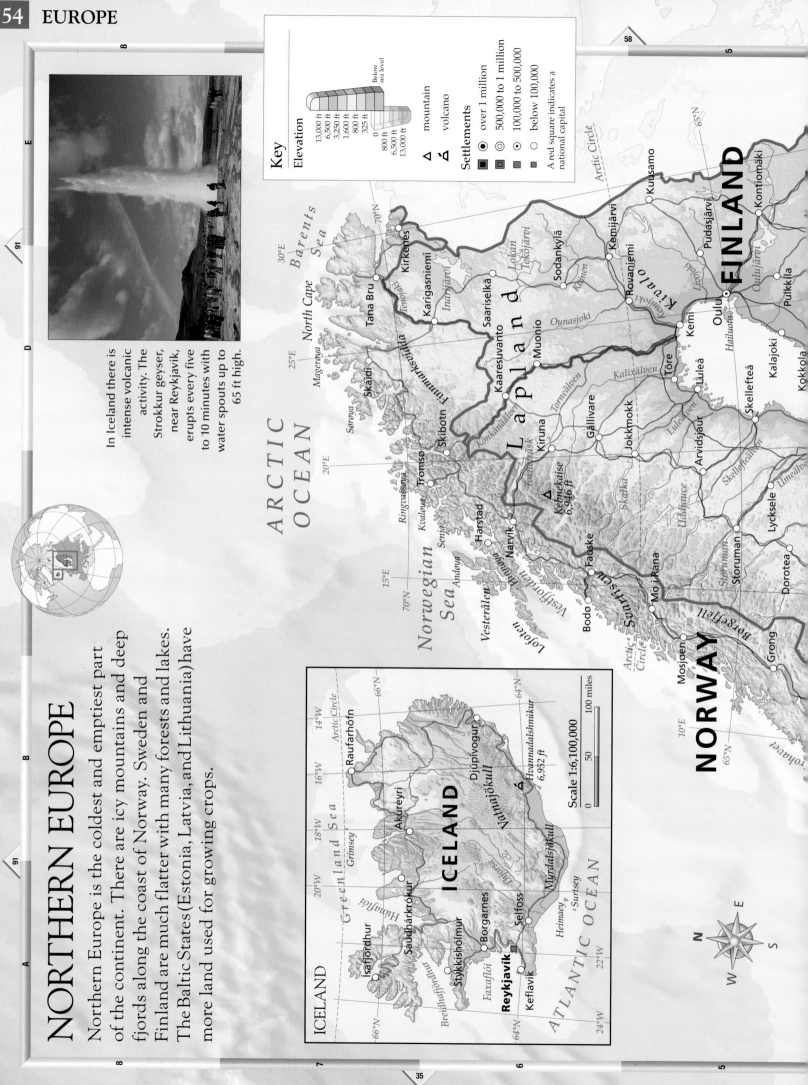

ARCTIC OCEAN

Barents Sea

North Cape

Magerøya

Søroya

Ringvassøya

Kvaløya

Senja

Andøya

Vesterålen

Lofoten

Norwegian Sea

30°E
25°E
20°E
15°E
70°N
70°N
65°N

Kirkenes
Kirkenes
Tana Bru
Karigasniemi
Skaidi
Saariselkä
Skibotn
Tromsø
Harstad
Narvik
Bodø
Fauske
Mo i Rana
Mosjøen
Grong

Kaaresuvanto
Kautokeino
Kiruna
Gällivare
Jokkmokk
Arvidsjaur
Storuman
Dorotea
Storman

Kebnekaise
6,946 ft

L a p l a n d

Lokan Tekojärvi
Inarijärvi
Sodankylä
Kemijärvi
Rovaniemi
Kemi
Oulu
Töre
Luleå
Skellefteå
Kalajoki
Kokkola

Kilpisjärvi
Karesuvanto
Muonio
Pulkkila
Pudasjärvi
Kuusamo
Kontiomäki

Kemijoki
Ounasjoki
Kalixälven
Torneälven
Luleälven
Skellefteälven
Umeälven
Ångermanälven
Indalsälven

Kitalo

Arctic Circle
Arctic Circle

NORWAY

FINLAND

Børgefjell

10°E
5
65°N
65°N

ICELAND

Greenland Sea

Grímsey

Ísafjördhur
Saudhárkrókur
Stykkishólmur
Borgarnes
Reykjavik
Keflavik
Selfoss
Akureyri
Raufarhöfn
Djúpivogur
Hvannadalshnúkur 6,952 ft

Vatnajökull
Mýrdalsjökull
Heimaey
Surtsey

ICELAND

ATLANTIC OCEAN

Hunaflói
Faxaflói
Breidhafjördhur
Breidhafjördhur

Arctic Circle

14°W
16°W
18°W
20°W
22°W
24°W
66°N
64°N
66°N
64°N

Scale 1:6,100,000

0   50   100 miles

N
W   E
S

8   91   91   B   A   D   E   58   5
7   35   6   5

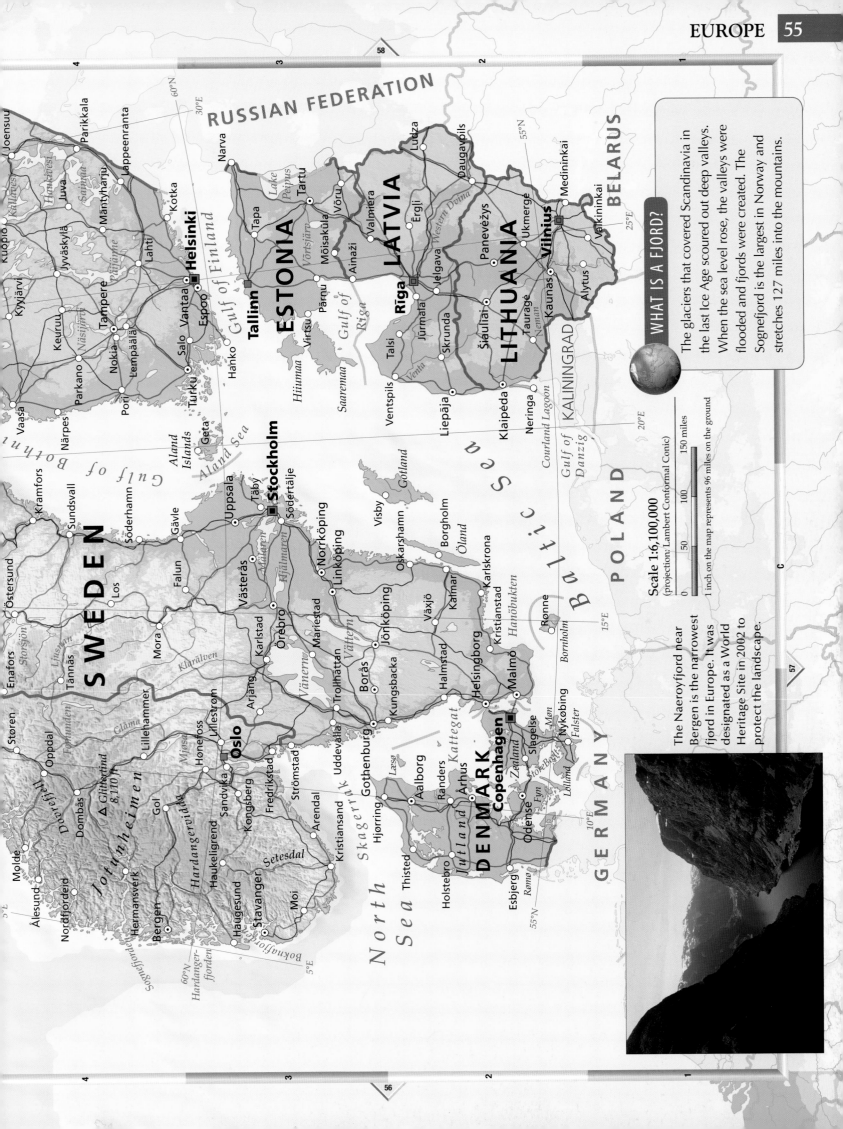

RUSSIAN FEDERATION

SWEDEN

Östersund
Storsjön
Enafors
Storen
Tännäs
Los
Oppdal
Dombås
Molde
Ålesund
Nordfjordeid
Hernansverk
Bergen
Haugesund
Stavanger
Moi
Setesdal
Kristiansand
Arendal
Strömstad
Fredrikstad
Sandvika
Kongsberg
Gol
Hardangervidda
Haukeligrend
Honefoss
Lillestrom
Oslo
Lillehammer
Hamar
Mjøsa
△ Glittertind 8,110 ft
Jotunheimen
Dovrefjell
Rondane
Forunden
Fardalen
Glåma
Klarälven
Mora
Falun
Arjäng
Karlstad
Örebro
Vänern
Västerås
Mälaren
Hjälmaren
Uppsala
Täby
Stockholm
Södertälje
Gävle
Söderhamn
Sundsvall
Kramfors
Ljusnan
Vättern
Trollhättan
Mariestad
Norrköping
Linköping
Borås
Jönköping
Kungsbacka
Gothenburg
Uddevalla
Växjö
Kalmar
Oskarshamn
Karlskrona
Kristianstad
Halmstad
Helsingborg
Malmö

Glittertind 8,110 ft

Sognefjorden
Hardanger-fjorden
Boknafjord
60°N
5°E

North Sea
Skagerrak
Kattegat

DENMARK

Hjorring
Aalborg
Thisted
Holstebro
Randers
Århus
Esbjerg
Ribe
Odense
Fyn
Svendborg
Slagelse
Jutland
Zealand
Copenhagen
Nyköbing
Lolland
Falster
Møn
Store Bælt
Læsø
55°N
10°E

GERMANY

POLAND

Ronne
Bornholm
Hanöbukten

Baltic Sea

15°E

FINLAND
Joensuu
Parikkala
Lappeenranta
Kallavesi
Mäntyharju
Juva
Haukivesi
Kuopio
Jyväskylä
Keuruu
Kyyjärvi
Saimaa
Savonlinna
Kotka
Lahti
Kouvola
Tampere
Nokia
Lempäälä
Näsijärvi
Päijänne
Helsinki
Vantaa
Espoo
Salo
Turku
Hanko
Pori
Parkano
Närpes
Vaasa
Gulf of Finland
60°N
30°E

Åland Islands
Geta
Åland Sea

Gulf of Bothnia

ESTONIA
Narva
Lake Peipus
Tapa
Tartu
Võru
Tallinn
Pärnu
Virtsu
Vôrtsjärv
Hiiumaa
Saaremaa
Gulf of Riga

LATVIA
Ludza
Daugavpils
Valmiera
Valga
Ērgļi
Mõisaküla
Ainaži
Rīga
Jūrmala
Talsi
Ventspils
Jelgava
Western Dvina
Liepāja
Skrunda
Venta
55°N
25°E

LITHUANIA
Šiauliai
Panevėžys
Ukmerge
Medininkai
Vilnius
Kaunas
Taurage
Neman
Alytus
Valkininkai
Klaipėda
Neringa
Courland Lagoon
KALININGRAD
Gulf of Danzig
20°E

BELARUS

Gulf of Bothnia

Baltic Sea

57

WHAT IS A FJORD?

The glaciers that covered Scandinavia in the last Ice Age scoured out deep valleys. When the sea level rose, the valleys were flooded and fjords were created. The Sognefjord is the largest in Norway and stretches 127 miles into the mountains.

Scale 1:6,100,000
(projection: Lambert Conformal Conic)

0   50   100   150 miles

1 inch on the map represents 96 miles on the ground

The Naeroyfjord near Bergen is the narrowest fjord in Europe. It was designated as a World Heritage Site in 2002 to protect the landscape.

WESTERN EUROPE

Western Europe faces the Atlantic Ocean.
Winds bring moist air from the southwest
to the rocky coasts of Great Britain, Ireland,
France, Spain, and Portugal. In the past,
mariners from these seafaring nations set
out to explore the world in sailing ships.
Today trade still dominates the economy
of western Europe, which is one of the
most prosperous areas in the world.

The dramatic limestone scenery of the
Dolomites in northern Italy attracts tourists
and skiers. Scientists believe recent rock falls
are partly the result of abnormal heating and
cooling linked to climate change.

Key

Elevation

13,000 ft	
6,500 ft	
3,250 ft	
1,600 ft	
800 ft	
325 ft	
0	Below
800 ft	sea level
6,500 ft	
13,000 ft	

Settlements

■ ⊙	over 1 million
▣ ◎	500,000 to 1 million
▪ ⊙	100,000 to 500,000
▪	below 100,000

A red square indicates a
national capital

△ mountain   ⌂ volcano

ATLANTIC OCEAN

Grampians
Aberdeen
Dundee
Glasgow • Edinburgh
UNITED
KINGDOM
Newcastle upon Tyne
Belfast
IRELAND
Isle of Man (to UK)
Leeds
Manchester
Liverpool • Sheffield
Dublin
Nottingham
Birmingham
Norwich
Cork
Oxford
Cardiff • London
Southampton
Brighton
Plymouth
English Channel
Lille
Channel Islands (to UK)
le Havre
Rouen
Seine
Paris
Rennes
Orléans
Loire
St. Nazaire • Nantes • Tours
FRANCE
Limoges
Massif Central
Bay of Biscay
Bordeaux
Garonne
A Coruña (La Coruña)
Gijón
Santander
Cordillera Cantábrica
Bilbao
Toulouse
Vigo
León
Pyrenees
ANDORRA
Burgos
Ebro
Oporto
Valladolid
Zaragoza
Barcelona
Salamanca
Coimbra
Madrid
Tarragona
PORTUGAL
Tagus
SPAIN
Mallorca
Lisbon
Valencia
Palma de Mallorca
Badajoz
Ibiza
Córdoba
Balearic Islands
Murcia
Seville
Granada
Cartagena
Mediterranean
Cádiz
Málaga
Gibraltar (to UK)

North Sea

N
W E
S

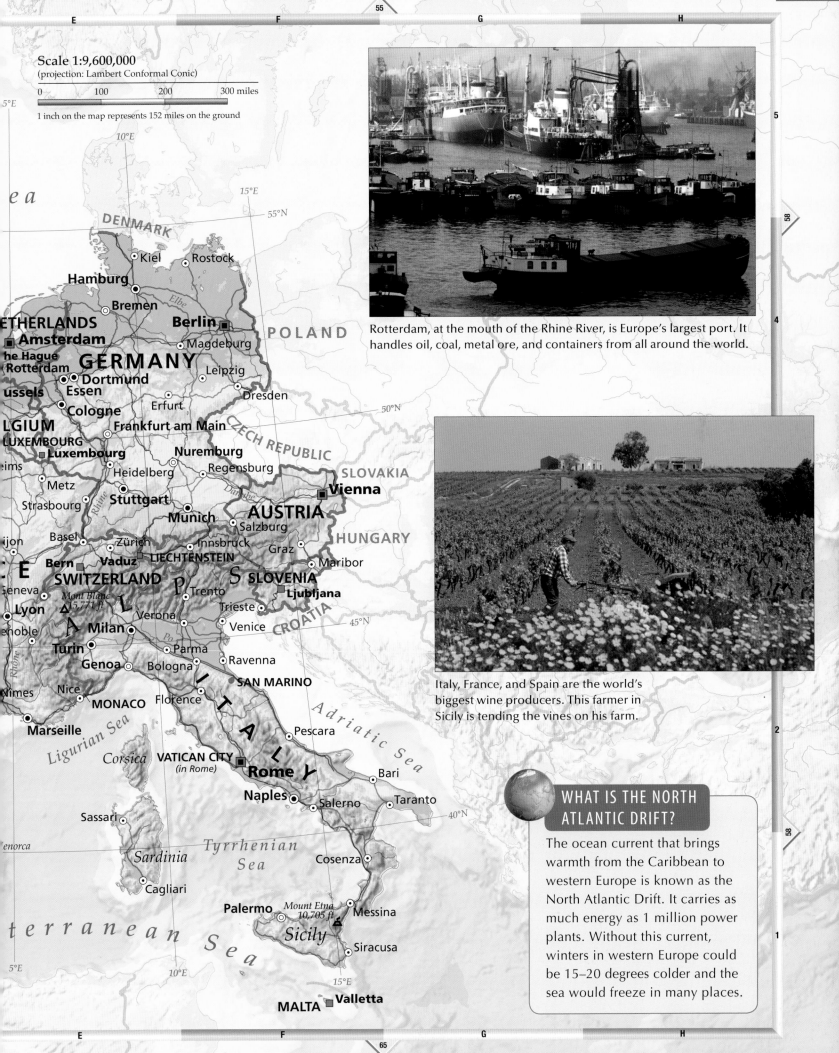

E F G H

Scale 1:9,600,000
(projection: Lambert Conformal Conic)

0   100   200   300 miles

1 inch on the map represents 152 miles on the ground

5°E

10°E

15°E

55°N

50°N

45°N

40°N

5°E

10°E

15°E

ea

DENMARK

Kiel   Rostock

Hamburg

Bremen   Elbe

Berlin

ETHERLANDS   POLAND

Amsterdam   Magdeburg

he Hague   GERMANY

Rotterdam   Leipzig

ussels   Dortmund

Essen   Dresden

LGIUM   Cologne   Erfurt

Frankfurt am Main   CZECH REPUBLIC

LUXEMBOURG

Luxembourg   Nuremburg

eims   Heidelberg   Regensburg   SLOVAKIA

Metz   Danube   Vienna

Strasbourg   Stuttgart   AUSTRIA

Rhine   Munich   Salzburg   HUNGARY

Basel   Innsbruck   Graz

jon   Zürich   Vaduz   LIECHTENSTEIN   Maribor

Bern   SLOVENIA

SWITZERLAND   Trento   Ljubljana

Geneva   Mont Blanc   Trieste

15,771 ft   Verona   Venice   CROATIA

Lyon   Milan   Po

enoble   Parma   Ravenna

Turin

Genoa   Bologna

Nimes   Nice   ITALY   SAN MARINO

MONACO   Florence   Adriatic Sea

Marseille   Pescara

Ligurian Sea

Corsica   VATICAN CITY   Rome

(in Rome)   Bari

enorca   Naples   Salerno   Taranto

Sardinia   Tyrrhenian   Sea

Sassari   Cosenza

Cagliari

terranean   Sea   Palermo   Mount Etna   Messina

10,705 ft

Sicily   Siracusa

MALTA   Valletta

Rotterdam, at the mouth of the Rhine River, is Europe's largest port. It handles oil, coal, metal ore, and containers from all around the world.

Italy, France, and Spain are the world's biggest wine producers. This farmer in Sicily is tending the vines on his farm.

WHAT IS THE NORTH ATLANTIC DRIFT?

The ocean current that brings warmth from the Caribbean to western Europe is known as the North Atlantic Drift. It carries as much energy as 1 million power plants. Without this current, winters in western Europe could be 15–20 degrees colder and the sea would freeze in many places.

EASTERN EUROPE

Romania, Poland, Ukraine, and the Russian Federation are the largest countries in eastern Europe. In Russia two great rivers, the Don and the Volga, thread their way to the sea past fields and factories. In southeast Europe, the Danube River links four capital cities on its journey from the edge of the Alps to the Black Sea. Many parts of eastern Europe have a continental climate with marked differences between summer and winter temperatures.

Many countries in eastern Europe have broken away from the Russian Federation. These crowds gathered in Kiev, Ukraine, in 2004 to challenge the results of an election.

One of the world's most beautiful Gothic gateways, the Charles Bridge in Prague attracts many tourists. It was built across the Vltava River in the 14th century by King Charles IV to link the old town with the castle on the other side of the river.

RUSSIAN FEDERATION

Ural Mountains

Kara Sea

Barents Sea

White Sea

Kola Peninsula

Novaya Zemlya

Ostrov Vaygach

Ostrov Kolguyev

Vorkuta

Nar'yan-Mar

Pechora

Ukhta

Syktyvkar

Severnaya Dvina

Archangel

Onega

Lake Onega

Petrozavodsk

Perm'

Kirov

Vologda

Cherepovets

Novgorod

Lake Ladoga

Saint Petersburg

ESTONIA

Lake Peipus

Murmansk

NORWAY

FINLAND

Arctic Circle

75°N

70°N

65°N

60°N

55°N

50°N

65°E

60°E

55°E

50°E

45°E

40°E

35°E

30°E

25°E

WHAT ARE THE STEPPES?

The grasslands that stretch across southern parts of the Russian Federation and Ukraine are known as the steppes. The flat land and thick black soil found here are ideal for farming wheat. As a result the steppes are known as the bread basket of Europe.

Key

Elevation

13,000 ft	
6,500 ft	
3,250 ft	
1,600 ft	
800 ft	
325 ft	
0	Below sea level
800 ft	
6,500 ft	
13,000 ft	

△ mountain

Settlements

- ◉ over 1 million
- ◎ 500,000 to 1 million
- ◉ 100,000 to 500,000
- ○ below 100,000

A red square indicates a national capital

Scale 1:13,600,000
(projection: Lambert Conformal Conic)

| 0 | 100 | 200 | 300 | 400 miles |

1 inch on the map represents 215 miles on the ground

Orsk
Samara
Orenburg
Ul'yanovsk
Tol'yatti
Balakovo
Saratov
Penza
Tambov
KAZAKHSTAN
Astrakhan'
Volgograd
Kamyshin
Volgodonsk
Grozny
Pyatigorsk
△ El'brus 18,510 ft
Caspian Sea
Caspian Depression
Volga
Don
Caucasus
GEORGIA
AZERBAIJAN
Krasnodar
Rostov-na-Donu
Sochi
Voronezh
Ryazan'
Tula
Oral
Kursk
Orël
MOSCOW
Novgorod
Vitsyebsk
Mahilyow
Homyel'
Syeverodonets'k
Donets'k
Dnipropetrovs'k
Kharkiv
Sumy
Mariupol'
Kerch
Kirovohrad
Melitopol'
Cherkasy
Simferopol'
Sevastopol'
Chernihiv
Kiev
UKRAINE
Polatsk
Minsk
BELARUS
Kaliningrad
Białystok
Pripet Marshes
Dnieper
Brest
Lublin
L'viv
Zhytomyr
Vinnytsya
Kishinau
MOLDOVA
Odesa
Black Sea
Constanţa
Istanbul
Burgas
TURKEY
Ploviv
BULGARIA
Pleven
Bucharest
ROMANIA
Braşov
Piteşti
Cluj-Napoca
Timişoara
Carpathian Mountains
HUNGARY
Budapest
Pécs
Osijek
Zagreb
CROATIA
SLOVENIA
AUSTRIA
Bratislava
SLOVAKIA
Košice
Kraków
Katowice
Olomouc
Łódź
Wrocław
Poznań
POLAND
Warsaw
Gdańsk
Szczecin
GERMANY
Prague
CZECH REPUBLIC
BOSNIA & HERZEGOVINA
Sarajevo
SERBIA
Belgrade
MONTENEGRO
Podgorica
Split
Adriatic Sea
Tirana
ALBANIA
MACEDONIA
Skopje
Sofia
Thessaloníki
Lárisa
GREECE
Athens
Pátra
Ionian Islands
Ionian Sea
Crete
Irákleio
Cyclades
Dodecanese
Mediterranean Sea
TURKISH REPUBLIC OF NORTHERN CYPRUS
(recognised only by Turkey)
Nicosia
CYPRUS
Limassol
Ual
50°N
60°E
55°E
45°N
50°E
45°E
40°E
35°E
30°E
25°E
20°E
15°E
40°N
35°N
45°N
50°N
Vinnytsya

AFRICA POLITICAL

There are 54 countries in Africa. Many African countries gained independence from Europe in the 1960s and 1970s. Although there have been frequent disputes since then, there have been few changes to the borders that were imposed at the time by colonial rulers.

New countries

In 1950, there were just four independent countries in Africa, but now all of the nations on the mainland are self-governing.

Key

■ capital city

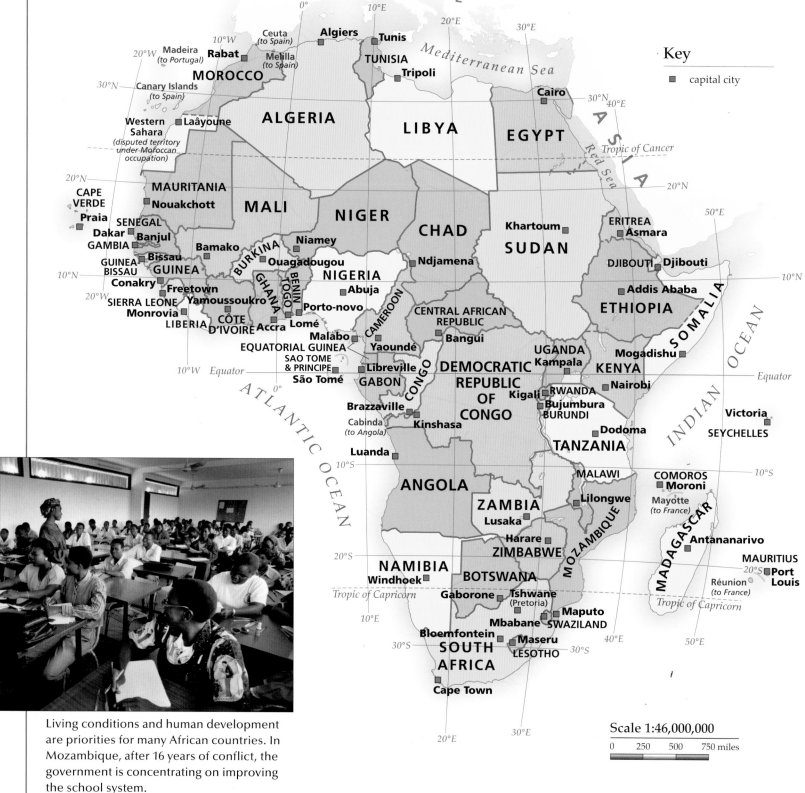

EUROPE

Ceuta (to Spain)
Algiers
Tunis
TUNISIA
Tripoli
Cairo
Mediterranean Sea
Madeira (to Portugal)
Rabat
Melilla (to Spain)
MOROCCO
Canary Islands (to Spain)
Western Sahara (disputed territory under Moroccan occupation)
Laâyoune
ALGERIA
LIBYA
EGYPT
Tropic of Cancer
Red Sea
ASIA
CAPE VERDE
Praia
Nouakchott
MAURITANIA
MALI
NIGER
CHAD
Khartoum
SUDAN
ERITREA
Asmara
SENEGAL
Dakar
Banjul
GAMBIA
Bamako
BURKINA
Niamey
Ndjamena
DJIBOUTI
Djibouti
GUINEA-BISSAU
Bissau
GUINEA
Ouagadougou
NIGERIA
Addis Ababa
Conakry
Freetown
Yamoussoukro
GHANA
BENIN
TOGO
Abuja
ETHIOPIA
SOMALIA
SIERRA LEONE
Monrovia
CÔTE D'IVOIRE
Accra
Lomé
Porto-novo
CAMEROON
CENTRAL AFRICAN REPUBLIC
LIBERIA
Malabo
Bangui
EQUATORIAL GUINEA
Yaoundé
UGANDA
Mogadishu
SAO TOME & PRINCIPE
Libreville
Kampala
KENYA
São Tomé
GABON
DEMOCRATIC REPUBLIC OF CONGO
RWANDA
Kigali
Nairobi
CONGO
Brazzaville
Bujumbura
BURUNDI
Victoria
Cabinda (to Angola)
Kinshasa
Dodoma
SEYCHELLES
Luanda
TANZANIA
INDIAN OCEAN
ATLANTIC OCEAN
ANGOLA
MALAWI
COMOROS
Moroni
Mayotte (to France)
ZAMBIA
Lilongwe
Lusaka
MOZAMBIQUE
MADAGASCAR
Antananarivo
Harare
MAURITIUS
ZIMBABWE
Réunion (to France)
Port Louis
NAMIBIA
BOTSWANA
Windhoek
Tshwane (Pretoria)
Gaborone
Maputo
Mbabane
SWAZILAND
Bloemfontein
Maseru
SOUTH AFRICA
LESOTHO
Cape Town
Tropic of Capricorn
Equator
Atlantic Ocean

Scale 1:46,000,000
0 250 500 750 miles

Living conditions and human development are priorities for many African countries. In Mozambique, after 16 years of conflict, the government is concentrating on improving the school system.

AFRICA PHYSICAL

Africa is the second largest continent. It stretches from the Mediterranean Sea to the Cape of Good Hope. Nearly all of Africa lies in the Tropics. Deserts, rain forests, and grasslands make up much of the landscape. In the south and east of the continent there are high plains where the sources of many of Africa's famous rivers are found.

AFRICA FACTS

HIGHEST MOUNTAIN: Mount Kilimanjaro 19,341 ft

LONGEST RIVER: Nile River 4,145 miles

BIGGEST LAKE: Lake Victoria 26,834 sq miles

BIGGEST ISLAND: Madagascar 224,534 sq miles

BIGGEST DESERT: Sahara Desert 3,474,919 sq miles

BIGGEST COUNTRY: Sudan 967,499 sq miles

SMALLEST COUNTRY: Seychelles 176 sq miles

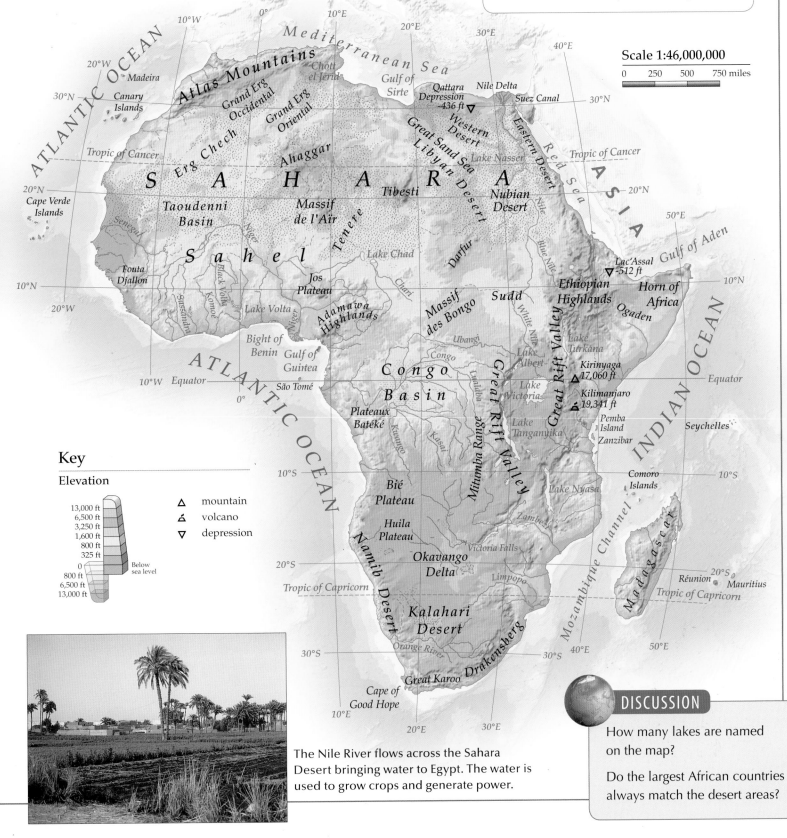

Scale 1:46,000,000

0   250   500   750 miles

Key

Elevation

13,000 ft
6,500 ft
3,250 ft
1,600 ft
800 ft
325 ft
0
800 ft
6,500 ft
13,000 ft

Below sea level

△ mountain
⏣ volcano
▽ depression

The Nile River flows across the Sahara Desert bringing water to Egypt. The water is used to grow crops and generate power.

DISCUSSION

How many lakes are named on the map?

Do the largest African countries always match the desert areas?

AFRICA FROM THE SKY

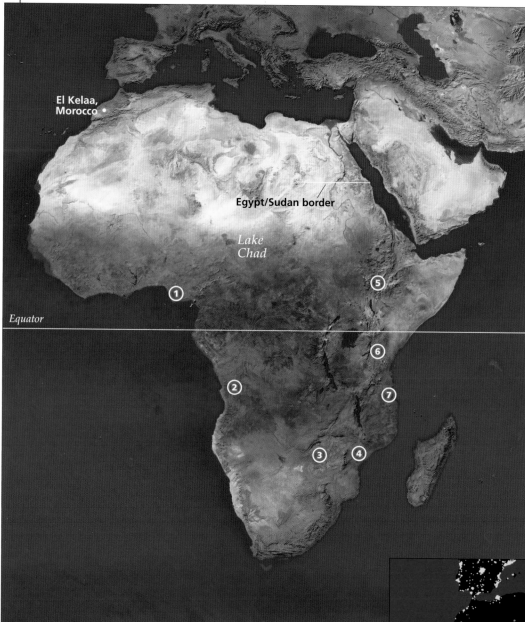

El Kelaa, Morocco •

Egypt/Sudan border

Lake Chad

Equator

Environmental hot spots

① Oil spills, Niger Delta, ongoing

② Landmines, Angola, ongoing

③ Drought, Zimbabwe, 2002, ongoing

④ Floods, Mozambique, 2000, 2001

⑤ Drought, Ethiopia, 1984, ongoing

⑥ Melting glaciers, Kilimanjaro, Tanzania, ongoing

⑦ Retreating mangrove forests, Tanzania, ongoing

The Sahara Desert stretches across northern Africa as a yellow band in this satellite image. The orange area in southwest Africa marks the Kalahari Desert. The rain forests and grasslands on each side of the equator show up in green. You can even trace the course of the Nile River as it threads its way to the Mediterranean Sea.

Africa at night

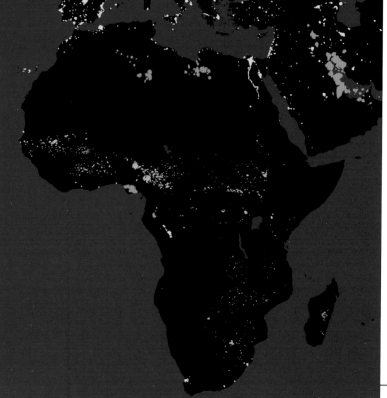

Flooding in Mozambique

February 2000

In this color-coded image, city lights are shown in yellow, oil flares in red, and forest fires in light purple. Note how few lights there are in Africa compared with southern Europe (at the top of the image).

The cyclones that hit Mozambique in 2000 and 2001 destroyed crops and made half a million people homeless.

Rose cultivation

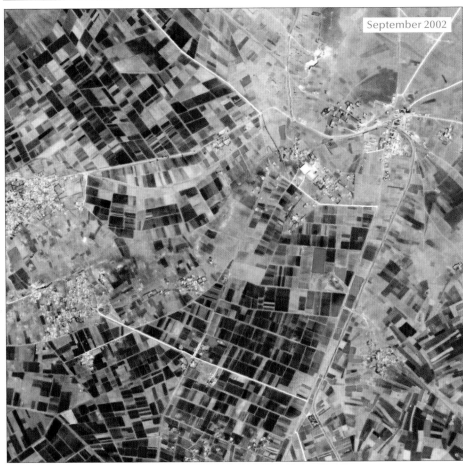

September 2002

The El Kelaa region of Morocco is famous for rose water. In this photograph, the rose fields are shown in green and red. You can see the settlements in pale blue.

Lake Chad

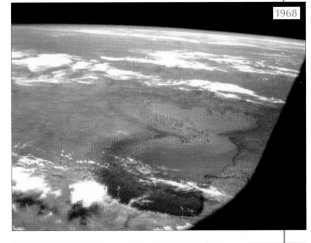

1968

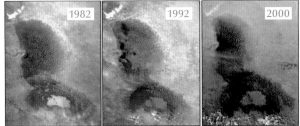

1982 1992 2000

Lake Chad lies in an internal drainage basin. Satellite images record how the lake has shriveled over the last few decades.

Sandstorm over Africa

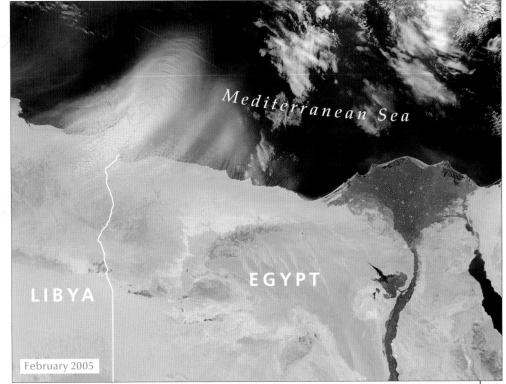

Mediterranean Sea

LIBYA

EGYPT

February 2005

Strong winds in the Sahara Desert sometimes whip up the sand and blow it into the sea. Note the Nile Delta and Red Sea on the eastern side of this image.

Fields in the desert

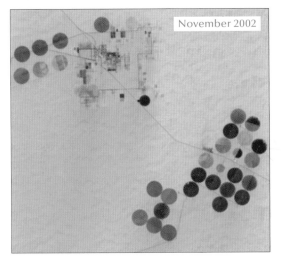

November 2002

These circular fields near the Egypt-Sudan border are irrigated with underground water. The water has taken thousands of years to accumulate, but is unlikely to last beyond 2050 if people continue to use the same amounts as they do at the moment.

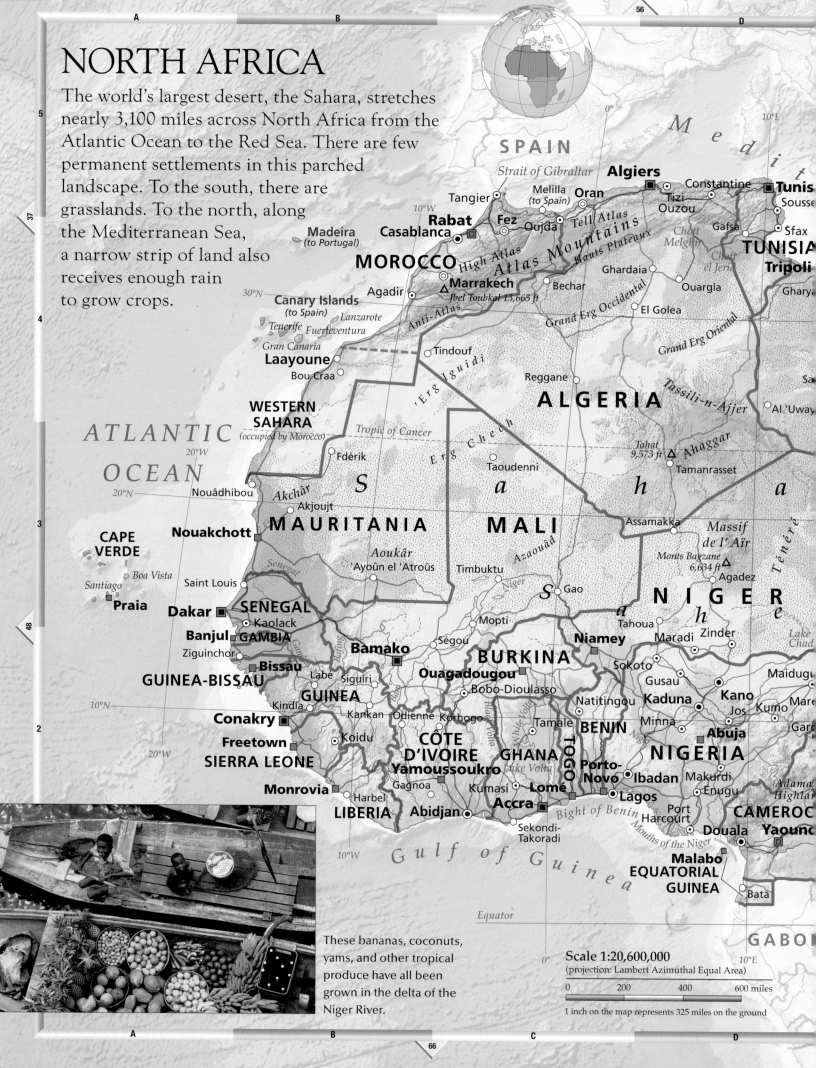

NORTH AFRICA

The world's largest desert, the Sahara, stretches nearly 3,100 miles across North Africa from the Atlantic Ocean to the Red Sea. There are few permanent settlements in this parched landscape. To the south, there are grasslands. To the north, along the Mediterranean Sea, a narrow strip of land also receives enough rain to grow crops.

SPAIN

Strait of Gibraltar
Tangier
Melilla (to Spain)
Algiers
Constantine
Tunis
Sousse
Oran
Tizi Ouzou
Rabat
Fez
Oujda
Tell Atlas
Gafsa
Sfax
Madeira (to Portugal)
Casablanca
High Atlas
Atlas Mountains
Hauts Plateaux
TUNISIA
Agadir
Marrakech
Jbel Toubkal 13,665 ft
Bechar
Ghardaia
Chott el Jerid
Tripoli
MOROCCO
Anti-Atlas
Ouargla
Ghary
Canary Islands (to Spain)
Lanzarote
Tenerife
Fuerteventura
Gran Canaria
Laayoune
Bou Craa
Tindouf
'Erg Iguidi
Reggane
El Golea
Grand Erg Occidental
Grand Erg Oriental
ALGERIA
Tassili-n-Ajjer
ATLANTIC
Tropic of Cancer
Fdérik
Erg Chech
Taoudenni
OCEAN
Tahat 9,573 ft
Ahaggar
Al 'Uway
Nouâdhibou
Akchâr
Tamanrasset
Akjoujt
S
a
h
a
Assamakka
Massif de l' Aïr
MAURITANIA
MALI
Aoukâr
Azaouâd
CAPE VERDE
Nouakchott
Monts Bagzane 6,634 ft
Boa Vista
Senegal
'Ayoûn el 'Atroûs
Timbuktu
Niger
S
Agadez
Santiago
Saint Louis
Gao
N I G E R
Ténéré
Praia
Dakar
SENEGAL
Mopti
a
Tahoua
Lake Chad
Kaolack
Ségou
h
Maradi
Zinder
Banjul
GAMBIA
Bamako
Niamey
e
Ziguinchor
BURKINA
Sokoto
Bissau
Labé
Siguiri
Ouagadougou
Gusau
Maidugu
GUINEA-BISSAU
Bobo-Dioulasso
Kaduna
Kano
Kindia
Natitingou
Jos
Kumo
Mare
Kankan
Minna
GUINEA
Odienné
Korhogo
Black Volta
Abuja
Gard
Conakry
Koidu
BENIN
NIGERIA
Tamale
Freetown
CÔTE
GHANA
TOGO
White Volta
SIERRA LEONE
D'IVOIRE
Porto-Novo
Ibadan
Makurdi
Yamoussoukro
Lake Volta
Lomé
Enugu
Adama Highlan
Monrovia
Gagnoa
Kumasi
Accra
Lagos
Harbel
Abidjan
Bight of Benin
Port Harcourt
CAMEROC
LIBERIA
Sekondi-Takoradi
Mouths of the Niger
Douala
Yaound
Gulf of Guinea
Malabo
EQUATORIAL GUINEA
Bata
Equator

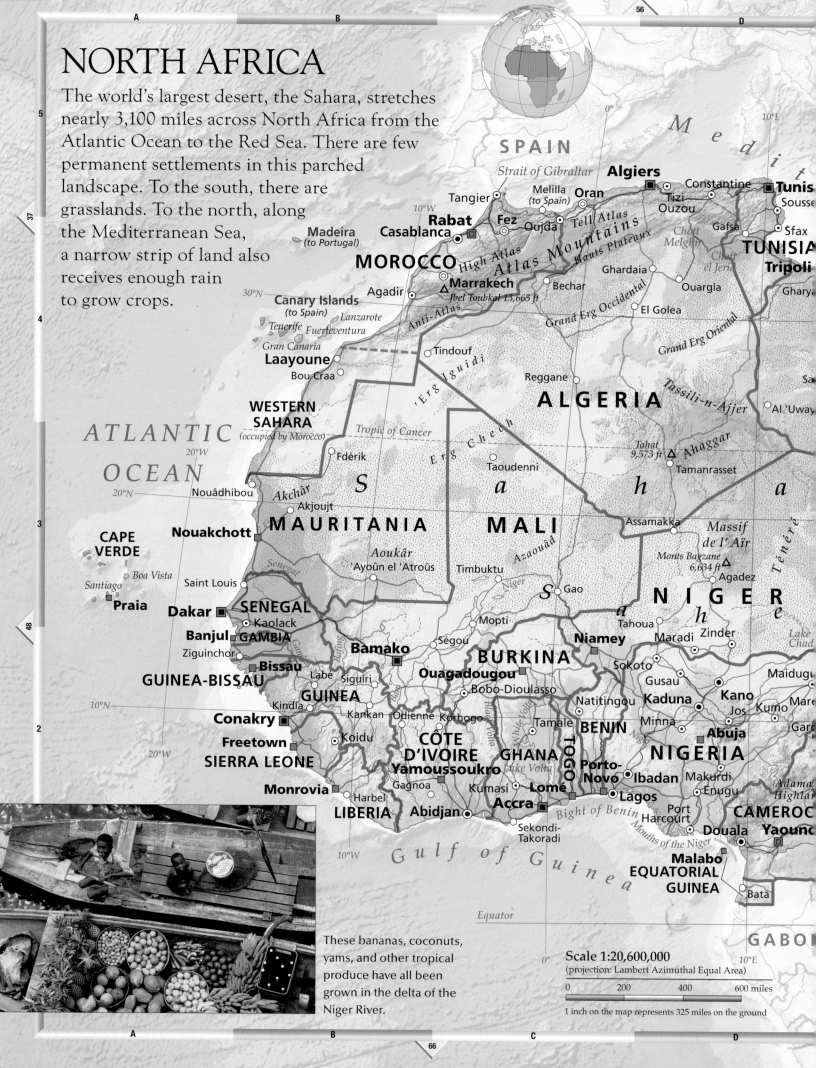

These bananas, coconuts, yams, and other tropical produce have all been grown in the delta of the Niger River.

Scale 1:20,600,000
(projection: Lambert Azimuthal Equal Area)

0   200   400   600 miles

1 inch on the map represents 325 miles on the ground

GABO

58

74

An oasis can vary from being just a few trees in the desert to a great city on an old trading route.

WHAT IS AN OASIS?

At some places in a desert, water that is trapped in underground rocks comes out on the surface. This creates an oasis. By moving from one oasis to another, nomads and travelers are able to survive in the harsh desert climate.

N
W E
S

E F 58 H

20°E

30°E CYPRUS

ranean Sea

Al Bayda'
Misratah
Tobruk
Gulf of Sirte
Benghazi
Alexandria
Nile Delta
ISRAEL
JORDAN
Port Said
Suez Canal
Suez
30°N
El Giza
Cairo
Sinai
Qattara Depression
Waddan
Jalu
El Minya
△ *Gebel Musa 7,497 ft*

LIBYA
Great Sand Sea
Asyut
EGYPT
El Kharga
Luxor
Libyan Desert
Red Sea
SAUDI ARABIA
40°E

Ramlat Rabyanah
Al Khufrah
Aswan
Lake Nasser
Tropic of Cancer

Pic Bette △ *7,500 ft*
Jabal al 'Uwaynát △ *a 6,257 ft*
Akasha
Nubian Desert
20°N
50°E

Tibesti r
Zouar
△ *Emi Koussi 11,204 ft*
El'Atrun
Port Sudan
YEMEN
Ennedi
Atbara
Faya
ERITREA
Kassala
Asmara
Lac' Assal 512 ft
Omdurman
Khartoum
Wad Medani
Aseb
Gulf of Aden
CHAD
Abéché
Darfur
El Fasher
SUDAN
Gedaref
Gonder
DJIBOUTI
Berbera
△ *Shimbiris 7,897 ft*
Raas Xaafuun
10°N
Ndjamena
El Obeid
Nyala
Bahir Dar
Lake Tana
Dese
Djibouti
Abuye Meda 13,123 ft △
Dire Dawa
SOMALIA
oundou
Sarh
Birao
Malakal
Ethiopian
Hargeysa
Garoowe
CENTRAL
Wau
Sudd
White Nile
Addis Ababa
Highlands
Ogaden
Shebeli
AFRICAN REPUBLIC
Bambari
Obo
Jima
ETHIOPIA
Negele
Beledweyne
erbérati
Bangui
Juba
Great Rift Valley
Juba
Bahr Aouk
Chari
Kotto
Bomu
Ubangi
Oubangui
Bouar
White Nile
Blue Nile
Atbara

DEM. REP. CONGO
UGANDA
Lake Turkana
KENYA
Marka
Mogadishu
20°E
30°E
Equator
Equator
Equator
Kismaayo
50°E
40°E

INDIAN OCEAN

Key

Elevation

13,000 ft
6,500 ft
3,250 ft
1,600 ft
800 ft
325 ft
0
800 ft
6,500 ft
13,000 ft
Below sea level

Settlements

■ ◉ over 1 million
▣ ◎ 500,000 to 1 million
▤ ⊙ 100,000 to 500,000
▪ ○ below 100,000

A red square indicates a national capital

△ mountain   ▽ depression

G H
67

SOUTHERN AFRICA

Much of southern Africa is 3,250 ft or more above sea level. It is famous for the wild animals that roam across the grasslands. Great rivers such as the Orange and Zambezi drain the uplands. There are valuable reserves of gold, copper, diamonds, and other minerals across the region. However, most of the wealth goes to other countries and southern Africa remains one of the poorest parts of the world.

The Victoria Falls on the Zambesi River are the largest curtain of water in the world (1 mile wide) and a UNESCO World Heritage Site.

The Great Rift Valley cuts across Tanzania with steep slopes along the sides and a valley up to 37 miles wide.

Scale 1:18,500,000
(projection: Lambert Azimuthal Equal Area)

| 0 | 200 | 400 | 600 miles |

1 inch on the map represents 292 miles on the ground

Key

Elevation

13,000 ft
6,500 ft
3,250 ft
1,600 ft
800 ft
325 ft
0
800 ft
6,500 ft
13,000 ft

Below sea level

Settlements

■ ⊙ over 1 million

▣ ◎ 500,000 to 1 million

▪ ⊙ 100,000 to 500,000

▪ ○ below 100,000

A red square indicates a national capital

△ mountain   ▽ depression

Map labels

CENTRAL AFRICAN REPUBLIC
Oubangui
Ubangi
Gemena
Bum
Ngoko
CAMEROON
Bitam
Ouésso
Lulonga
GABON
CONGO
Mbandaka
Congo Bas
DEMOC
REPU
OF CO
Makoua
Ik
EQUATORIAL GUINEA
SAO TOME AND PRINCIPE
São Tomé
Equator
Libreville
Port-Gentil
Moanda
Ogooué
Lac Ntomba
Kwa
Plateaux Batéké
Bandundu
Mangai
Sant
Setté Cama
Dolisie
Brazzaville
Kinshasa
Kikwit
Ilebo
Pointe-Noire
Boma
Kananga
Cabinda (to Angola)
Matadi
Tshikapa
ATLANTIC OCEAN
Luanda
N'Dalatando
Saurimo
10°S
ANGOLA
Dilolo
Lobito
Benguela
Môco 8,593 ft △
Luena
Huambo
Bié Plateau
Zamb
Lungué-Bun
Namibe
Lubango
Menongue
Mor
Tombua
Huíla Plateau
Cubango
Caprivi Strip
Cunene
Olifa
Oshikango
Okava
Delt
10°E
Etosha Pan
Grootfontein
20°S
NAMIBIA
BO
Brandberg 8,445 ft △
Karibib
Gha
Walvis Bay
Windhoek
Tropic of Capricorn
Kalaha
Mariental
Desert
Keetmanshoop
Molo
Lüderitz
Groot Karasberg
Oranjemund
Orange River
30°S
SOUT
Vanrhynsdorp
St. Helena Bay
Beau
Gre
Cape Town
Cape of Good Hope
20°E
20°E
10°E
64

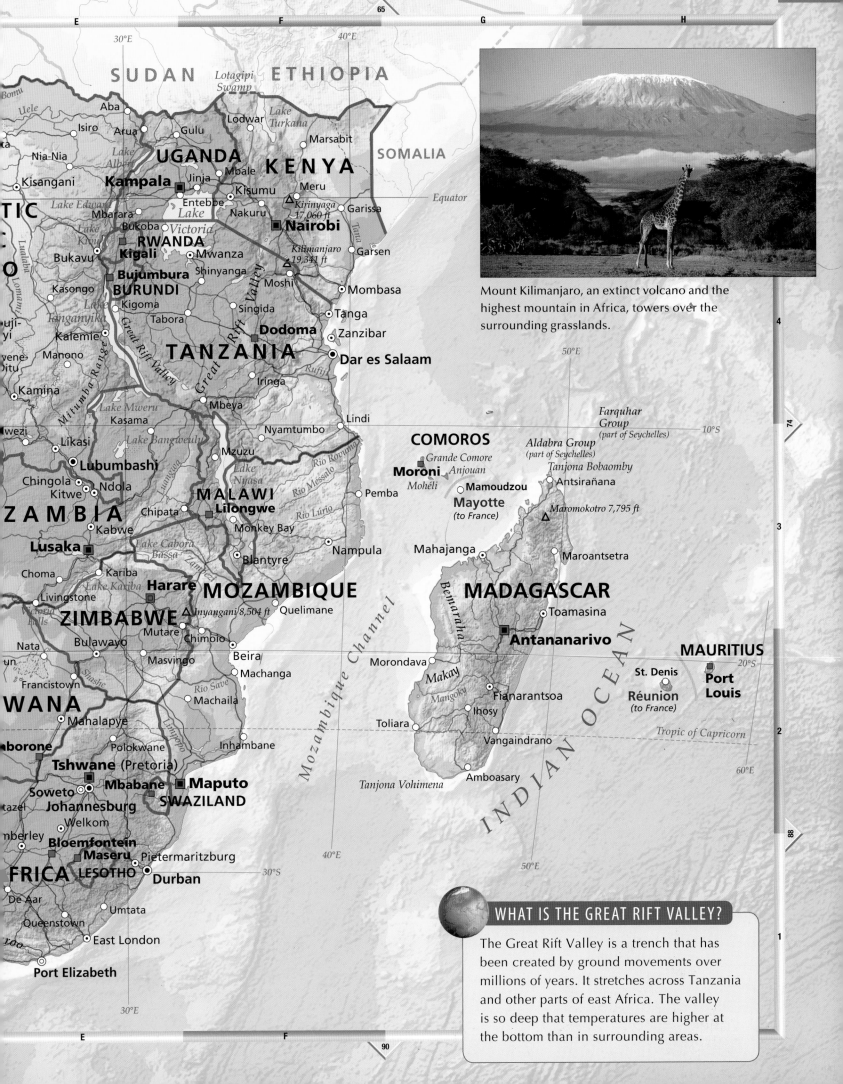

Mount Kilimanjaro, an extinct volcano and the highest mountain in Africa, towers over the surrounding grasslands.

WHAT IS THE GREAT RIFT VALLEY?

The Great Rift Valley is a trench that has been created by ground movements over millions of years. It stretches across Tanzania and other parts of east Africa. The valley is so deep that temperatures are higher at the bottom than in surrounding areas.

ASIA POLITICAL

Home to many ancient civilizations, Asia is divided into 49 countries. Although the Russian Federation is biggest in terms of area, India, China, Pakistan, Indonesia, and Bangladesh all have larger populations. There are many border disputes and the Middle East (the area to the south of Turkey) has seen decades of conflict.

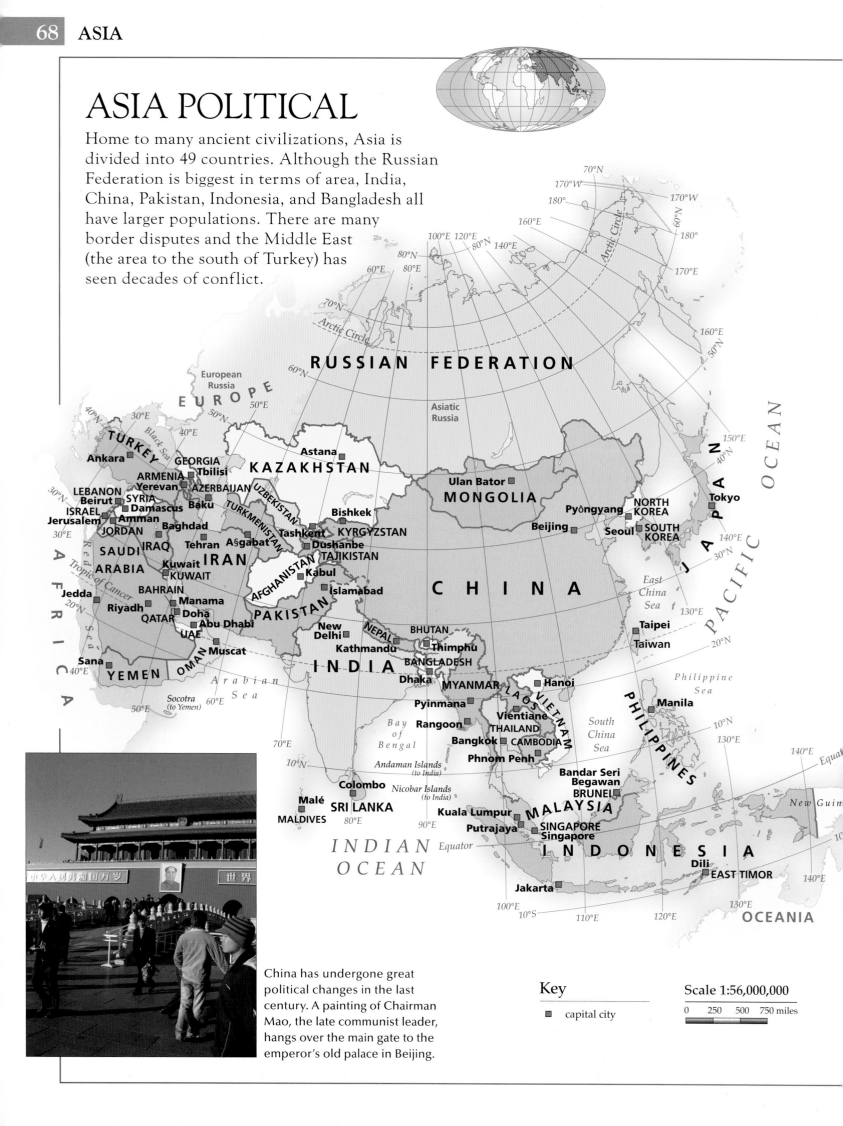

China has undergone great political changes in the last century. A painting of Chairman Mao, the late communist leader, hangs over the main gate to the emperor's old palace in Beijing.

Key

■ capital city

Scale 1:56,000,000

0   250   500   750 miles

ASIA PHYSICAL

Asia is the world's biggest continent. It is larger than Europe and Africa combined. Rivers flow from the high plateau of Tibet through forests and plains to the surrounding oceans. The heart of Asia is a desert region, including the famous Gobi and Takla Makan. The southern and eastern fringe of Asia is dotted with islands.

ASIA FACTS

HIGHEST MOUNTAIN: Mount Everest 29,035 ft

LONGEST RIVER: Yangtze 3,964 miles

BIGGEST LAKE: Caspian Sea 143,244 sq miles

BIGGEST ISLAND: Borneo 290,001 sq miles

BIGGEST DESERT: Arabian desert 888,035 sq miles

BIGGEST COUNTRY: Russian Federation 6,592,772 sq miles

SMALLEST COUNTRY: Maldives 116 sq miles

The Yangtze River cuts through deep gorges on its way to the East China Sea. Despite opposition, large dams are being built along the river to generate electricity.

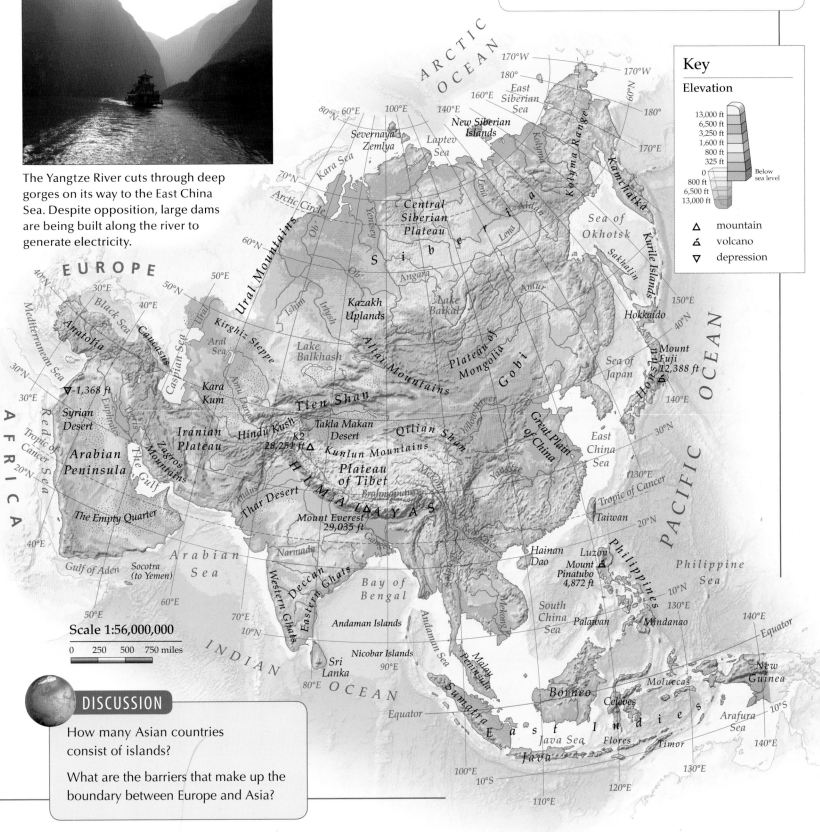

Key

Elevation

13,000 ft
6,500 ft
3,250 ft
1,600 ft
800 ft
325 ft
0
800 ft
6,500 ft
13,000 ft
Below sea level

△ mountain
⌂ volcano
▽ depression

Scale 1:56,000,000

0   250   500   750 miles

DISCUSSION

How many Asian countries consist of islands?

What are the barriers that make up the boundary between Europe and Asia?

ASIA FROM THE SKY

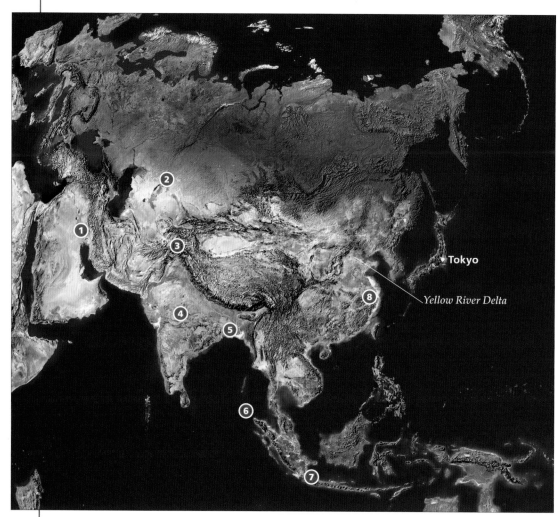

• Tokyo

Yellow River Delta

Environmental hot spots

① Gulf war oil fires, Iraq, 1991

② Water loss, Aral Sea, ongoing

③ Earthquake, Pakistan, 2005

④ Chemical explosion, Bhopal, India, 1984

⑤ Floods, Bangladesh, 1998

⑥ Tsunami, Banda Aceh, Indonesia, 2004

⑦ Forest fires, Indonesia, 1997

⑧ Polluted cities, China, ongoing

The deserts of Saudi Arabia and central Asia are shown in brown on this image. To the north, the green areas depict the forests of Siberia and tundra around the Arctic Ocean.

Asia at night

Oil fires in the Gulf

February 1991

The smoke from fires set off in the Gulf War polluted the snow in the Himalayas more than 2,000 miles to the east. This photograph shows an oil field set on fire by troops.

The cities of India, China, and Japan show up brightly in this night image. Tibet and western China, mostly being uninhabited, remain in the dark. The lights of Europe appear in the top left-hand corner.

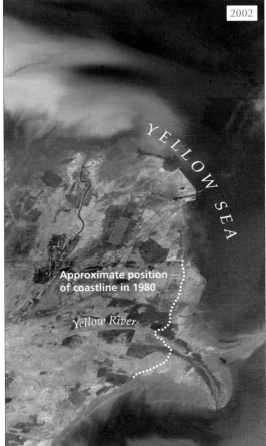

Yellow River Delta

The Yellow River in China carries huge quantities of silt down to the sea. This image shows how much the delta has grown in 22 years.

The growth of Tokyo

Tokyo has grown from a population of around 1.5 million in 1860 to 35 million today. The built-up area, shown here in gray blue, has extended across lowland areas to the north and west of the historic core.

Tsunami damage

This image of northwest Indonesia was taken before the 2004 tsunami. Much of the area is forested, with fields and villages in the lowlands. The beaches show up clearly in white.

This image was taken after the tsunami. The brown areas show the deforestation and damage caused by severe flooding. Debris has changed the color of the sea around the coastline.

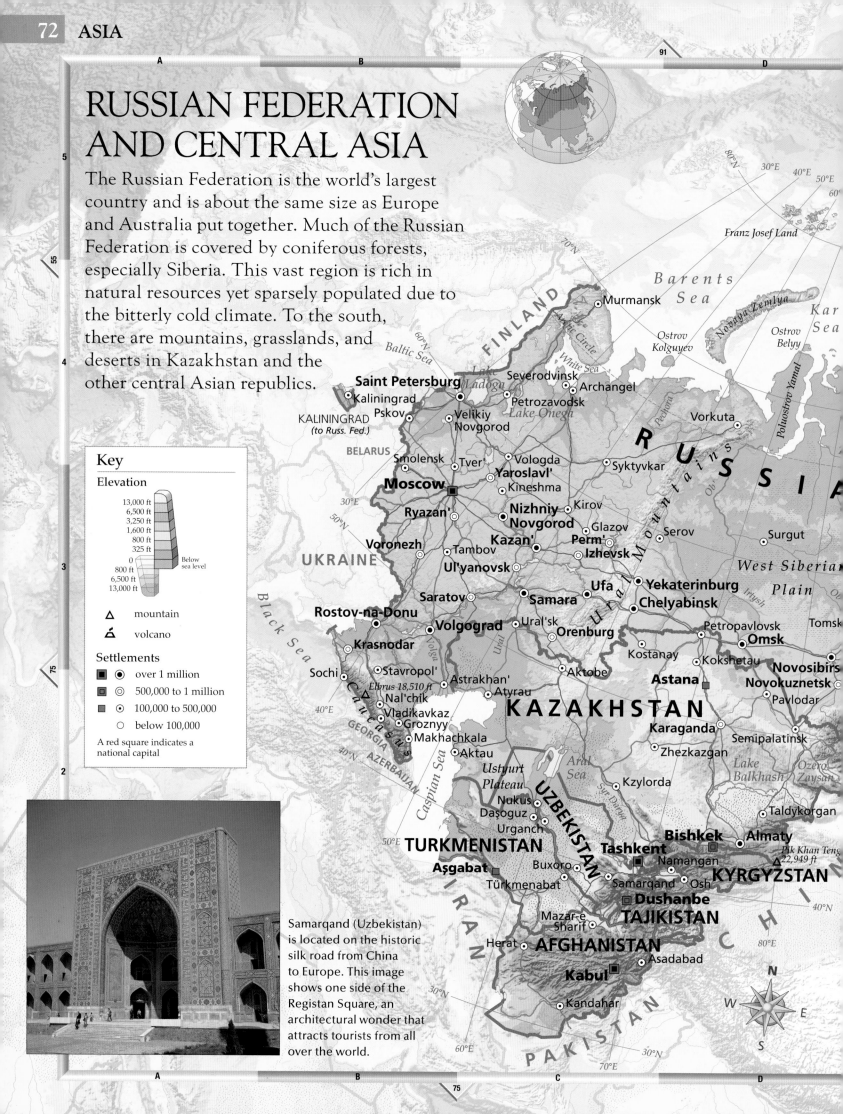

RUSSIAN FEDERATION AND CENTRAL ASIA

The Russian Federation is the world's largest country and is about the same size as Europe and Australia put together. Much of the Russian Federation is covered by coniferous forests, especially Siberia. This vast region is rich in natural resources yet sparsely populated due to the bitterly cold climate. To the south, there are mountains, grasslands, and deserts in Kazakhstan and the other central Asian republics.

Key

Elevation

13,000 ft
6,500 ft
3,250 ft
1,600 ft
800 ft
325 ft
Below sea level
800 ft
6,500 ft
13,000 ft

△ mountain
⬙ volcano

Settlements

■ ⊙ over 1 million
▨ ◎ 500,000 to 1 million
▧ ⊙ 100,000 to 500,000
○ below 100,000

A red square indicates a national capital

Samarqand (Uzbekistan) is located on the historic silk road from China to Europe. This image shows one side of the Registan Square, an architectural wonder that attracts tourists from all over the world.

Franz Josef Land

Barents Sea

Novaya Zemlya
Ostrov Kolguyev
Ostrov Belyy
Kar Sea

FINLAND
Murmansk
Arctic Circle
Poluostrov Yamal

Baltic Sea
Severodvinsk
Archangel
Lake Ladoga
Saint Petersburg
Petrozavodsk
Kaliningrad
Pskov
Velikiy Novgorod
Lake Onezh
Vologda
Syktyvkar
Vorkuta

KALININGRAD (to Russ. Fed.)
BELARUS
Smolensk
Tver'
Yaroslavl'
Kineshma
Moscow
Ryazan'
Nizhniy Novgorod
Kirov
Glazov
Perm'
Izhevsk
Serov
Surgut

R U S S I A

Ural Mountains
Ob'
Pechora

UKRAINE
Voronezh
Tambov
Kazan'
Ul'yanovsk
Ufa
Yekaterinburg
Chelyabinsk
West Siberian Plain
Irtysh
Tomsk

Saratov
Samara
Ural'sk
Orenburg
Petropavlovsk
Omsk
Novosibirsk

Black Sea
Rostov-na-Donu
Volgograd
Volga
Ural
Aktobe
Kostanay
Kokshetau
Novokuznetsk
Pavlodar

Krasnodar
Sochi
Elbrus 18,510 ft
Stavropol'
Nal'chik
Astrakhan'
Atyrau
Astana
Karaganda
Semipalatinsk

Caucasus
Vladikavkaz
Groznyy
Makhachkala
Aktau
KAZAKHSTAN
Zhezkazgan
Lake Balkhash
Ozero Zaysan

GEORGIA
AZERBAIJAN
Caspian Sea
Ustyurt Plateau
Aral Sea
Kzylorda
Taldykorgan

Nukus
Daşoguz
Urganch
UZBEKISTAN
Syr Darya
Bishkek
Almaty

TURKMENISTAN
Aşgabat
Buxoro
Tashkent
Namangan
Pik Khan Tengri 22,949 ft
KYRGYZSTAN

Türkmenabat
Samarqand
Osh
Dushanbe
TAJIKISTAN
CHINA

Mazar-e Sharif
AFGHANISTAN
Herat
Asadabad
Kabul
Kandahar

I R A N
P A K I S T A N

N
W   E
S

E F 91 G H

170°W
Bering Strait
Chukchi
Sea
Wrangel
Island
180°
East
Siberian Sea
170°E
160°E
150°E
140°E
130°E
120°E
110°E
100°E
90°E
80°N
New Siberian
Islands
Ostrov
Kotel'nyy
Cherskiy
Chukot
Range
Gulf of
Anadyr
Bering
Sea
Anadyr'
Koryak Range
170°W
180°

Severnaya
Zemlya
October
Revolution
Island
Laptev
Sea
Poluostrov Taymyr
Ozero
Taymyr
North Siberian Lowland
Tiksi
Verkhoyanskiy Khrebet
Khrebet Cherskogo
Kolyma
Kolyma Range
Ostrov Karaginskiy
170°E
60°N

Noril'sk
Central
Siberian
Plateau
Kotuy
Lena
Magadan
Kamchatka
Vulkan Klyuchevskaya
Sopka 15,584 ft
Petropavlovsk-
Kamchatskiy
50°N

F E D E R A T I O N
Vilyuy
Yakutsk
Khrebet Dzhugdzhur
Sea of
Okhotsk
Ostrov
Paramushir
160°E

S i b e r i a
Aldan
Suntar
Kurile Islands

Yenisey
Zeya Reservoir
Sakhalin
Ostrov Iturup
3

Ust'-Ilimsk
Yablonovyy Khrebet
Tynda
Komsomol'sk-na-Amure
Amur
Yuzhno-Sakhalinsk
Ostrov Kunashir
150°E

Kansk
Bratsk
Lake
Baikal
Khabarovsk

nerovo
Krasnoyarsk
Chita
CHINA
Blagoveshchensk

rnaul
Irkutsk
Ulan-Ude
Lake Khanka
Ussuriysk
140°E

...ha
33 ft
...ai Mountains
Vladivostok
Nakhodka
Sea of
Japan
(East Sea)

MONGOLIA
120°E
110°E
130°E

100°E
90°E

Scale 1:27,000,000
(projection: Lambert Azimuthal Equal Area)

0   250   500   750 miles

1 inch on the map represents 426 miles on the ground

Trees are unable
to survive the
intense cold of
the tundra.

WHAT IS TUNDRA?

In northern areas of the Russian
Federation there are large marshy
areas called tundra. Here, despite
a brief summer, the soil beneath
the surface stays frozen all year
long. Water collects in marshes
on the flat land.

WESTERN ASIA AND THE MIDDLE EAST

Turkey and Iran are rugged, mountainous countries. Farther south, Syria and Iraq are hotter and drier with deserts that extend to the tip of the Arabian peninsula. The world's largest oil and gas fields are found here. As a result this region plays a crucial part in the world economy.

Like much of the city of Sana, Yemen, the summer palace (Dar al-Hajar) perches on top of rocks.

Baku, on the Caspian Sea, has important oil reserves. However, since the area is landlocked, the oil has to be exported by pipeline. There is widespread pollution around the derricks.

Map labels

59

30°E   35°E

BULGARIA   *Black Sea*

İstanbul   Zonguldak   Samsun

40°N   İzmit   Trabzı

GREECE   Balıkesir   Bursa   Ankara   Sivas

İzmir   *Anatolia*   TURKE

Kütahya   Malatya

Aydın   N

Konya   Gaziante

Antalya   Adana

35°N   Antakya   Alepp

30°E   Al Ladhiqiyah   SYRIA

CYPRUS   Tripoli   Hims

Mediterranean   Beirut

Sea   LEBANON   Damascu

Haifa   *Syria*

Tel Aviv-Yafo   Irbid   *Dese*

Jerusalem   Amman

Be'er Sheva   *Dead Sea*

30°N   ISRAEL JORDAN

Gulf of Suez   Jabal al Lawz
△ 8,465 ft

Tabūk   A

EGYPT   Dubā

35°E   25°N

Medina

Tropic of Cancer

Red Sea   Jedda

SUDAN   Mecca

20°N

WHAT IS IRRIGATION?

When it is too dry to grow crops, people sometimes bring water from other places. This is called irrigation. In the past, great civilizations grew up along the banks of rivers like the Tigris and Euphrates, which provided water for irrigation. Today water remains a key resource in the Middle East and the cause of potential conflict.

ERITREA

RUSSIAN FEDERATION

Sokhumi
GEORGIA
umi K'ut'aisi
Tbilisi
Vanadzor Ganca **Baku**
Yerevan ARMENIA
AZERBAIJAN
Mount Ararat
16,854 ft AZERBAIJAN
ake Van Van *Kühhā-ye*
arbakir *Sabalan* 15,784 ft Ardabil
Tabriz *Lake Urmia* Rasht
Maragheh Āmol
Mosul Zanjan *Qolleh-ye Damavand*
Kirkuk Hamadan **Karaj** 18,606 ft **Tehran**
Kermānshāh Qom Kashan
R A Q
Baghdad
An Najaf Dezful **Isfahan** Yazd
Euphrates **Ahvaz**
Basra
Ha'il Bushire
Kuwait
KUWAIT
afūd
Buraydah
Al Jubayl
Aẓ Ẓahran
BAHRAIN
Manama
QATAR
Al Hufuf **Doha**
Abu Dhabi
Riyadh
UNITED ARAB
EMIRATES
A U D I   A R A B I A
Peninsula
Arabian
Abha
Najran
Sharūrah
Salalah
YEMEN
Sana
Sayhut
Hodeida
Jabal Thamar
8,248 ft Al Mukalla
Ta'izz
Aden
DJIBOUTI

TURKMENISTAN

Caspian Sea

Gorgān **Mashhad**
Sabzevar

Dasht-e Kavir

I R A N

Kerman

AFGHANISTAN

Zahedan

PAKISTAN

Īrānshahr

Zagros Mountains

Shiraz

The Persian Gulf

Bandar-e 'Abbas

Strait of Hormuz

Jāsk

Sharjah

Dubai Al Fujayrah
Ar Rustaq **Muscat**

Gulf of Oman

Tropic of Cancer

O M A N

Sur

The Empty Quarter

I N D I A N   O C E A N

Gulf of Aden

Socotra
(to Yemen)

Scale 1:13,200,000
(projection: Lambert Conformal Conic)

0 100 200 300 400 miles

1 inch on the map represents 208 miles on the ground

SOUTH ASIA

South Asia is bounded by the Himalayas to the north, and seas and oceans in other directions. Three great rivers, the Indus, Ganges, and Brahmaputra, provide water from the mountains for farming on the plains. Nearly a quarter of the world's population lives in this region. Although there are many large cities, most people still live in traditional villages.

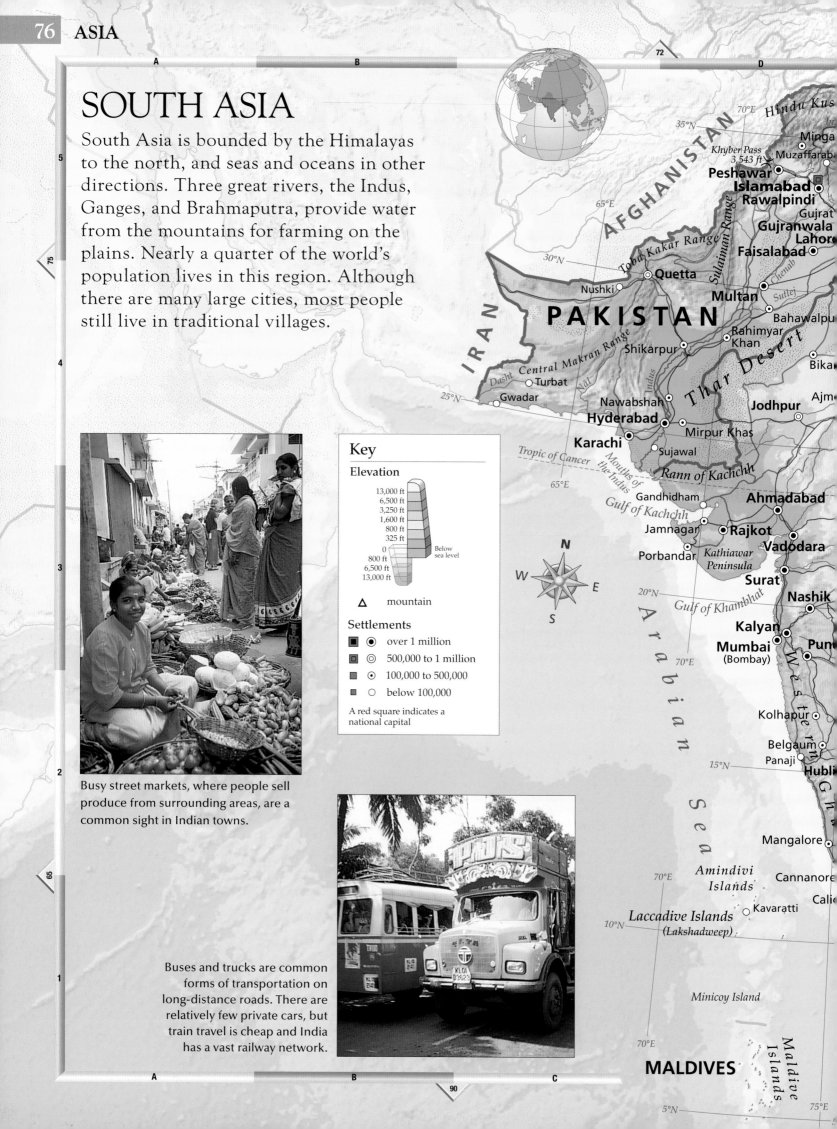

Busy street markets, where people sell produce from surrounding areas, are a common sight in Indian towns.

Buses and trucks are common forms of transportation on long-distance roads. There are relatively few private cars, but train travel is cheap and India has a vast railway network.

Key

Elevation

13,000 ft
6,500 ft
3,250 ft
1,600 ft
800 ft
325 ft
0
Below sea level
800 ft
6,500 ft
13,000 ft

△   mountain

Settlements

■ ⦿   over 1 million
▣ ◎   500,000 to 1 million
▪ ⊙   100,000 to 500,000
▪ ○   below 100,000

A red square indicates a national capital

AFGHANISTAN

Hindu Kus

Khyber Pass
3,543 ft

Minga

Muzaffarab

Peshawar
Islamabad
Rawalpindi

Gujrat

Gujranwala
Lahore

Faisalabad

IRAN

Toba Kakar Range

Sulaiman Range

Quetta

Nushki

Chenab

Multan

Sutlej

Bahawalpu

PAKISTAN

Rahimyar
Khan

Bika

Central Makran Range

Shikarpur

Thar Desert

Dasht

Turbat

Nal

Gwadar

Nawabshah

Jodhpur

Ajm

Hyderabad

Mirpur Khas

Indus

Karachi

Sujawal

Tropic of Cancer

Mouths of the Indus

Rann of Kachchh

65°E

Gandhidham

Ahmadabad

Gulf of Kachchh

Jamnagar

Rajkot

Vadodara

Porbandar

Kathiawar
Peninsula

Surat

Nashik

Gulf of Khambhat

Kalyan

Mumbai
(Bombay)

Pun

Arabian Sea

Kolhapur

Belgaum

Panaji

Hubli

Mangalore

Amindivi
Islands

Cannanore

Cali

Laccadive Islands
(Lakshadweep)

Kavaratti

Minicoy Island

Maldive Islands

MALDIVES

70°E
35°N
65°E
30°N
25°N
20°N
15°N
10°N
5°N
75°E

N
W E
S

The road from Pakistan to China follows an ancient route and climbs to 15,400 ft to cross the Himalayas.

K2
28,251 ft

Tianshuihai
35°N
80°E

nagar

mu

ritsar

Ludhiana

Chandigarh

Dehra Dun

eerut

lhi

New Delhi   Bareilly

Agra

aipur

Gwalior

ota   Jhansi

Allahabad

Bhopal   Jabalpur

ore

Khandwa

usawal

Nagpur   Raipur

mravati

Chandrapur

nded

Warangal

olapur   Hyderabad

Kurnool

Anantapur   Nellore

Cuddapah

Bangalore   Chennai (Madras)

ysore   Krishnagiri   Kanchipuram

Salem   Pondicherry

Coimbatore

Tiruchchirappalli

Madurai

ochin   Jaffna

Quilon

Tuticorin   Mannar

Trivandrum   Trincomalee

Nagercoil   Batticaloa

Gulf of Mannar   Negombo   Kandy

SRI LANKA

Colombo

Galle
80°E

CHINA

HIMALAYA
NEPAL

Salyan   **Kathmandu**

Lalitpur

Lucknow

Gorakhpur   Shiliguri

Kanpur   Dinajpur

Patna

Varanasi

Ganges

Dhanbad   Asansol

Ranchi   Jessore

Jamshedpur   **Kolkata**
(Calcutta)

Bilaspur

Sambalpur   Baleshwar

Mahanadi

Bhubaneshwar

Jagdalpur   Brahmapur

Eastern Ghats   Srikakulam

Visakhapatnam

Rajahmundry

Vijayawada

Machilipatnam

Kavali
15°N

Annapurna
26,545 ft

Mount Everest
29,035 ft

Kula Kangri
24,783 ft

BHUTAN
Thimphu

Brahmaputra

Dibrugarh

Jorhat

Guwahati

Shillong

Rangpur

Rajshahi   Sylhet

BANGLADESH

Dhaka

Khulna   **Chittagong**

Mouths of the Ganges

Imphal

Silchar

Aizawl

Tropic of Cancer

MYANMAR

20°N

85°E

B a y   o f
B e n g a l

I N D I A N
O C E A N

10°N

85°E   90°E

30°N

85°E   90°E   95°E

25°N

95°E

WHAT IS THE MONSOON?

Life in India, China, and parts of southeast Asia depends on the monsoon. The monsoon is a period of heavy rain that spreads inland from the ocean. Before the monsoon arrives, temperatures soar and the land becomes parched. When it breaks, the rain brings the temperature down and provides the water for plants to grow.

Andaman Islands
(to India)

North Andaman

Middle Andaman

Port Blair
South Andaman

Little Andaman

Ten Degree Channel

Car Nicobar

Nicobar Islands
(to India)

Katchall Island

Great Nicobar
Bananga
Indira Point
95°E

Andaman Sea

95°E
10°N

82

Scale 1:14,000,000
(projection: Lambert Conformal Conic)

0   100   200   300   400 miles

1 inch on the map represents 221 miles on the ground

E   78   H

F   90   G   H

CHINA AND MONGOLIA

The most crowded part of China is in the east. Here there are many big cities and fertile farmland. Mongolia and central areas of China are dominated by the barren Gobi desert. In the west, the plateau of Tibet forms the most extensive mountain area in the world and is the source of many great rivers.

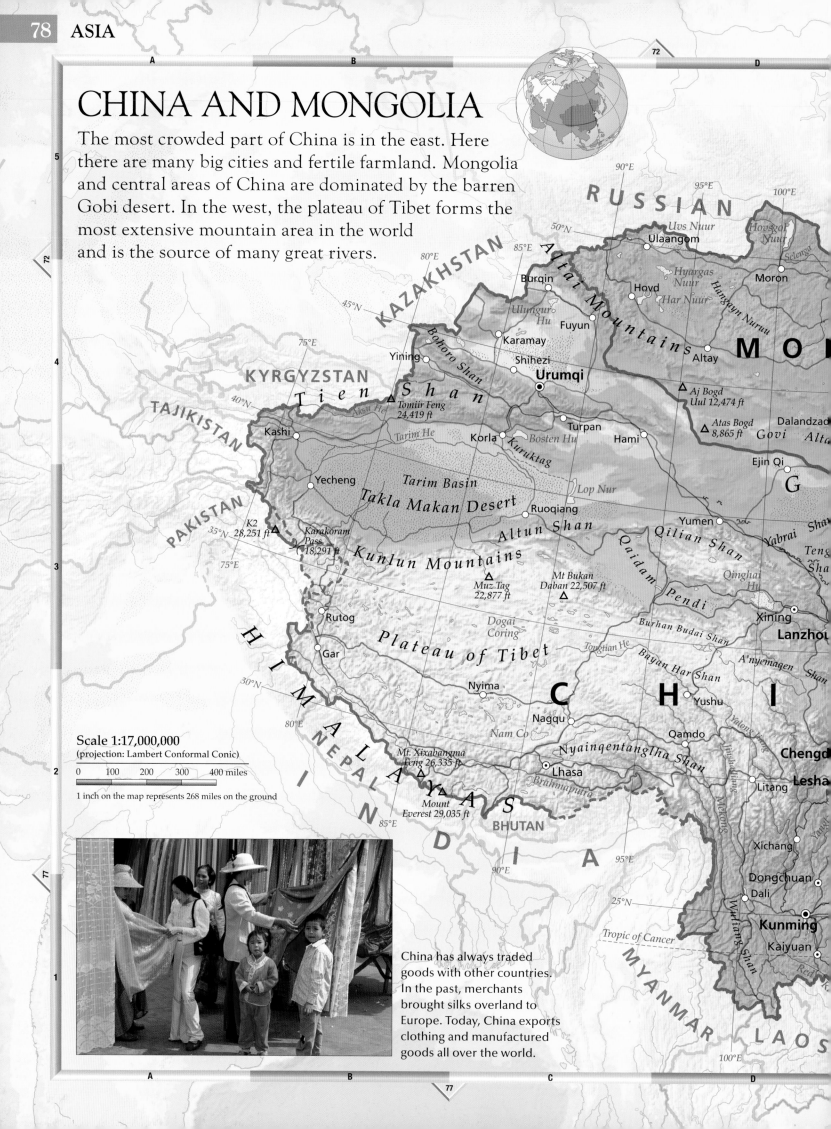

Scale 1:17,000,000
(projection: Lambert Conformal Conic)

0 100 200 300 400 miles

1 inch on the map represents 268 miles on the ground

China has always traded goods with other countries. In the past, merchants brought silks overland to Europe. Today, China exports clothing and manufactured goods all over the world.

E F 73 G H

N
E
S

FEDERATION

115°E

110°E

120°E

Mohe

125°E

130°E

50°N 135°E

Amur

Xiao Hinggan Ling

Great Khingan Range

Nen Jiang

Fuyuan

135°E

Sühbaatar

Darhan

Manzhouli

Hulun
Nur

Onon Gol

Zalantun

Jagdaqi

Qiqihar

Jiamusi

Jixi

45°N

Lake
Khanka

Ulan Bator

Choybalsan

Harbin

Kerulen

Ondorhaan

MONGOLIA

Menengiyn Tal

Baicheng

Mudanjiang

Manchuria

Jilin

Yanji

Ussuri

Xilinhot

Tongliao

Changchun

Erenhot

Chifeng

Fuxin

Shenyang

130°E

40°N

Chengde

Anshan

NORTH
KOREA

Hohhot

Beijing

Dandong

Baotou

Datong

Tangshan

Korea
Bay

Yinchuan

Tianjin

Dalian

SOUTH
KOREA

Yellow
River

Shijiazhuang

Yantai

Bo Hai

Great Wall of China

Taiyuan

Weifang

Yellow
Sea

Tongchuan

Handan

Jinan

Qingdao

125°E

Zhengzhou

Jining

Linyi

35°N

Tianshui

Luoyang

Xuzhou

Xi'an

Yancheng

CHINA

Hongze Hu

Nanjing

East China Sea

Han Shui

Hefei

Shanghai

Sichuan
Pendi

Yangtze

Wuhan

Tai Hu

Hangzhou

30°N

Wanxian

Yichang

Ningbo

Chongqing

Dongting Hu

Poyang Hu

Jingdezhen

Jinhua

Nanchang

Wenzhou

Zunyi

Changsha

Fuzhou

Huaihua

Pingxiang

Panzhihua

Hengyang

Fuzhou

Guiyang

Ganzhou

Yong'an

Taipei

25°N

Anshun

Yongzhou

T'aichung

Tropic of Cancer

Guilin

Shaoguan

Longyan

Taiwan Strait

Taiwan

Liuzhou

Hezhou

Xiamen

T'ainan

Bose

Guangzhou

Shantou

Taiwan

Nanning

Zhaoqing

Dongguan

Kaohsiung

Yulin

Hong Kong

VIETNAM

Beihai

Maoming

South China
Sea

120°E

Luzon Strait

Zhanjiang

115°E

Gulf of
Tongking

20°N

PHILIPPINES

20°N

Haikou

Hainan Dao

110°E

F 82 G

Key

Elevation

13,000 ft
6,500 ft
3,250 ft
1,600 ft
800 ft
325 ft
0
800 ft
6,500 ft
13,000 ft

Below
sea level

△ mountain

Settlements

■⊙ over 1 million
◙ 500,000 to 1 million
⊙ 100,000 to 500,000
○ below 100,000

A red square indicates a
national capital

There are 34 cities in China with a population of over 1 million people. Shanghai is the largest city with 17 million inhabitants. As cities grow larger, air and water pollution have become a serious problem.

WHY DO DESERTS SPREAD?

The land on the edge of a desert usually receives very little rain. If people cut down trees or overuse the land, the desert may spread. Desertification is a serious threat in many parts of the world. In China, dust from the Gobi Desert often blows as far as the capital city, Beijing.

KOREA AND JAPAN

Japan consists of four main islands and over 3,000 smaller ones. More than three-quarters of the land is taken up by high, volcanic mountains so most people live crowded together on the coastal plains. Japan is a major industrial nation with global car and electronics industries. On the mainland, South Korea has also developed high-tech and manufacturing industries. North Korea, which has a communist government, remains isolated from the rest of the world.

Key

Elevation

13,000 ft
6,500 ft
3,250 ft
1,600 ft
800 ft
325 ft
0
800 ft   Below
6,500 ft   sea level
13,000 ft

△ mountain

▲ volcano

Settlements

■ ⊙ over 1 million

◎ 500,000 to 1 million

⊙ 100,000 to 500,000

○ below 100,000

A red square indicates a
national capital

This great square in the center of Pyongyang is
used for parades and celebrations.

Map labels:

CHINA
RUSSIAN FEDERATION
Hoeryŏng
Paektu-san 9,022 ft △
Najin
Huch'ang
Hyesan
Ch'ŏngjin
Kanggye
Kimch'aek
Sinuiju
Huich'ŏn
Chongju
Sinp'o
Hamhung
Korea Bay
Sinmi-do
Wonsan
East Korea Bay
Pyŏngyang
NORTH KOREA
Namp'o
Kosong
Sariwon
(Ceasefire line since 1953)
Haeju
Sokch'o
Ongjin
Ch'unch'on
Kaesong
Kangnung
Inch'on
Seoul
Tonghae
Suwon
Wonju
Liancourt Rocks (disputed)
Ch'onan
Ch'ungju
SOUTH KOREA
Yellow Sea
Taejon
Andong
Oki-shoto
Kunsan
Dozen
Chŏnju
Taegu
P'ohang
Matsue
Kwangju
Ulsan
Mokp'o
Chinju
Pusan
Sunch'on
Koje-do
Korea Strait
Chin-do
Namhae-do
Tsushima
Masuda
Chugoku-sanchi
Okayama
Kogum-do
Ko-saki
Hiroshima
Cheju-do
Yamaguchi
Kitakyushu
Matsuyama
Niiha
Fukuoka
Iyo-nada
Shikoku
Sasebo
Kurume
Oita
Uwajima
Goto-retto
Kumamoto
Nagasaki
Nakamura
Amakusa-nada
Yatsushiro
Nobeoka
Koshikijima-retto
Kyushu
Sendai
Miyazaki
East China Sea
Kagoshima
Miyakonojō
Shibushi-wan
Tanega-shima
Yaku-shima

Taedong-gang
Yalu
Nangnim-sanmaek
Hamgyong-sanmaek
Taebaek-sanmaek
Sobaek-sanmaek

130°E
125°E
40°N
35°N
30°N

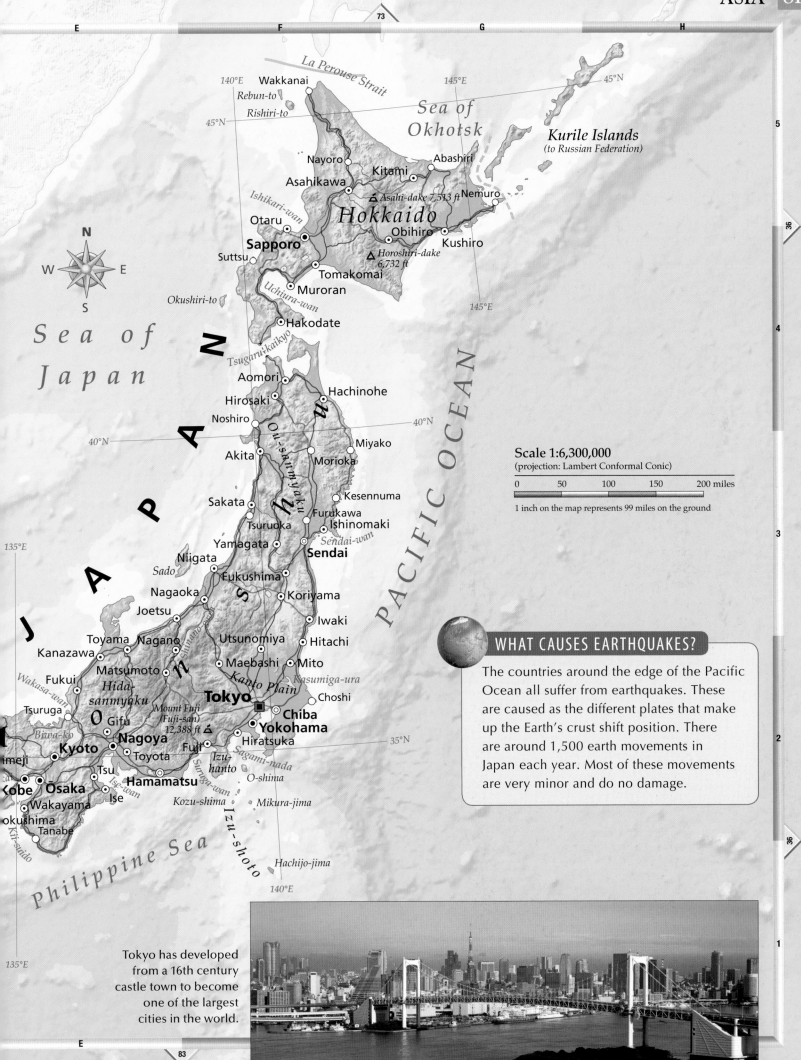

73

E   F   G   H

La Perouse Strait

140°E   Wakkanai   145°E   45°N

Rebun-to

45°N   *Rishiri-to*   Sea of Okhotsk   Kurile Islands
(to Russian Federation)

Nayoro   Kitami   Abashiri

Asahikawa   Nemuro

Ishikari-wan   ▲ *Asahi-dake 7,513 ft*   Hokkaido

Otaru   Obihiro   Kushiro

Sapporo

Suttsu   *Horoshiri-dake*
6,732 ft

Tomakomai

Uchiura-wan   Muroran

Okushiri-to   Hakodate

5

36

4

N

W   E

S

Tsugaru-kaikyo

S e a o f   Aomori

J a p a n   Hirosaki   Hachinohe

Noshiro   40°N

40°N   Akita   Miyako

Morioka

Sakata   Kesennuma

Furukawa

Tsuruoka   Ishinomaki

Yamagata   *Sendai-wan*

Niigata   **Sendai**

Sado   Fukushima

Nagaoka   Koriyama

Joetsu   Iwaki

Toyama   Nagano   Utsunomiya   Hitachi

Kanazawa   Maebashi   Mito

Matsumoto   Kanto Plain   *Kasumiga-ura*

Fukui   *Hida-sanmyaku*   **Tokyo**

Tsuruga   *Mount Fuji
(Fuji-san)*   Choshi
12,388 ft ▲

Gifu   Fuji   **Chiba**
Yokohama

Biwa-ko   Toyota   Hiratsuka

Nagoya   *Izu-hanto*   35°N

Kyoto   Tsu

imeji   **Hamamatsu**   *Sagami-nada*

Ise-wan   Ise   *Suruga-wan*   *O-shima*

Kobe   **Osaka**   *Kozu-shima*   *Mikura-jima*

Wakayama   *Izu-shoto*

okushima   Tanabe   *Kii-suido*

Hachijo-jima

135°E   P h i l i p p i n e S e a   140°E

135°E

J A P A N

PACIFIC OCEAN

Ou-sanmyaku

145°E

3

2

1

Scale 1:6,300,000
(projection: Lambert Conformal Conic)

0   50   100   150   200 miles

1 inch on the map represents 99 miles on the ground

WHAT CAUSES EARTHQUAKES?

The countries around the edge of the Pacific Ocean all suffer from earthquakes. These are caused as the different plates that make up the Earth's crust shift position. There are around 1,500 earth movements in Japan each year. Most of these movements are very minor and do no damage.

Tokyo has developed from a 16th century castle town to become one of the largest cities in the world.

SOUTHEAST ASIA

Rain forests once covered the lowland areas of Southeast Asia. Many of these forests have now been cleared to create space for farming, factories, and houses. Indonesia is the biggest and most populous country in the region. It is over 3,000 miles across and made up of more than 13,000 islands. Philippines is another island nation with modern industries.

Key

Elevation

13,000 ft
6,500 ft
3,250 ft
1,600 ft
800 ft
325 ft
0
800 ft
6,500 ft
13,000 ft

Below sea level

Settlements

■⊙ over 1 million
◎ 500,000 to 1 million
▪⊙ 100,000 to 500,000
▪○ below 100,000

A red square indicates a national capital

△ mountain

🜂 volcano

Singapore, the smallest country in Asia, has developed from a port into a major industrial city.

Scale 1:18,200,000
(projection: Mercator)

0	100	200	300	400	500 miles

1 inch on the map represents 287 miles on the ground

As well as creating a unique habitat, the dense vegetation of the rain forest protects the soil from erosion in heavy rain.

Buddhism is widespread in Southeast Asia. The temples attract visitors from all over the world.

WHAT IS AN ARCHIPELAGO?

An archipelago is a group or chain of islands. Some archipelagos are the tops of flooded mountain ranges. Others, such as Philippines, have been raised up from the ocean floor due to Earth's movements or volcanic activity.

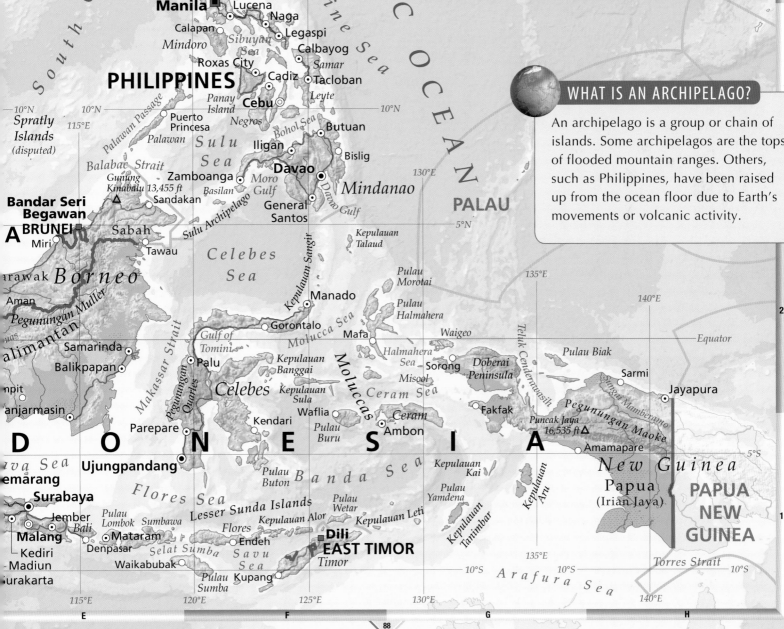

PACIFIC OCEAN

South China Sea

Luzon Strait

20°N

Babuyan Channel

20°N

racel Islands (disputed)

Luzon

Cordillera Central

Ilagan

Dagupan

Mount Pinatubo 4,872 ft △

Cabanatuan

15°N

Manila ■

Lucena

Naga

Calapan

Legaspi

Mindoro

Sibuyan Sea

Calbayog

Roxas City

Samar

PHILIPPINES

Cadiz

Tacloban

Panay Island

Cebu ◎

Leyte

10°N

10°N

Negros

Bohol Sea

Spratly Islands (disputed)

Puerto Princesa

Butuan

Palawan

Iligan

Bislig

Palawan Passage

Sulu Sea

Balabac Strait

Gunung Kimabalu 13,455 ft △

Zamboanga

Moro Gulf

Davao ●

Mindanao

130°E

Basilan

Davao Gulf

PALAU

Bandar Seri Begawan

Sandakan

Sulu Archipelago

General Santos

5°N

A

BRUNEI

Sabah

Kepulauan Talaud

Miri

Tawau

Celebes Sea

arawak

Borneo

Kepulauan Sangir

Aman

Pulau Morotai

Pegunungan Muller

Manado

Pulau Halmahera

135°E

140°E

as

alimantan

Gorontalo

Molucca Sea

Mafa

Waigeo

Equator

Samarinda

Gulf of Tomini

Halmahera Sea

Sorong

Doberai Peninsula

Pulau Biak

mpit

Balikpapan

Palu

Kepulauan Banggai

Misool

Sarmi

anjarmasin

Celebes

Kepulauan Sula

Ceram Sea

Fakfak

Jayapura

D

O

N

E

Waflia

Ceram

Puncak Jaya 16,535 ft △

Peguunungan Maoke

Kendari

Pulau Buru

Ambon

S

I

A

Parepare

Amamapare

5°S

Ujungpandang

Pulau Buton

Banda Sea

Kepulauan Kai

New Guinea

iva Sea

Papua (Irian Jaya)

PAPUA NEW GUINEA

emarang

Flores Sea

Pulau Yamdena

Surabaya

Pulau Lombok

Sumbawa

Lesser Sunda Islands

Pulau Wetar

Kepulauan Leti

Kepulauan Aru

Jember

Bali

Flores

Kepulauan Alor

Kepulauan Tanimbar

Malang

Mataram

Endeh

Dili

Kediri

Denpasar

Selat Sumba

Savu Sea

EAST TIMOR

Madiun

Waikabubak

Timor

Torres Strait

urakarta

Pulau Sumba

Kupang

10°S

Arafura Sea

10°S

OCEANIA POLITICAL

Australia is by far the largest and most populous country in Oceania. Like New Zealand, it was once a British colony but it has been independent for more than 100 years. To the north, Papua New Guinea is another significant country. To the east, there are numerous island states dotted across the Pacific Ocean.

Key

■ capital city
□ dependency capital city

Scale 1:56,000,000

0   400   800   1,200 miles

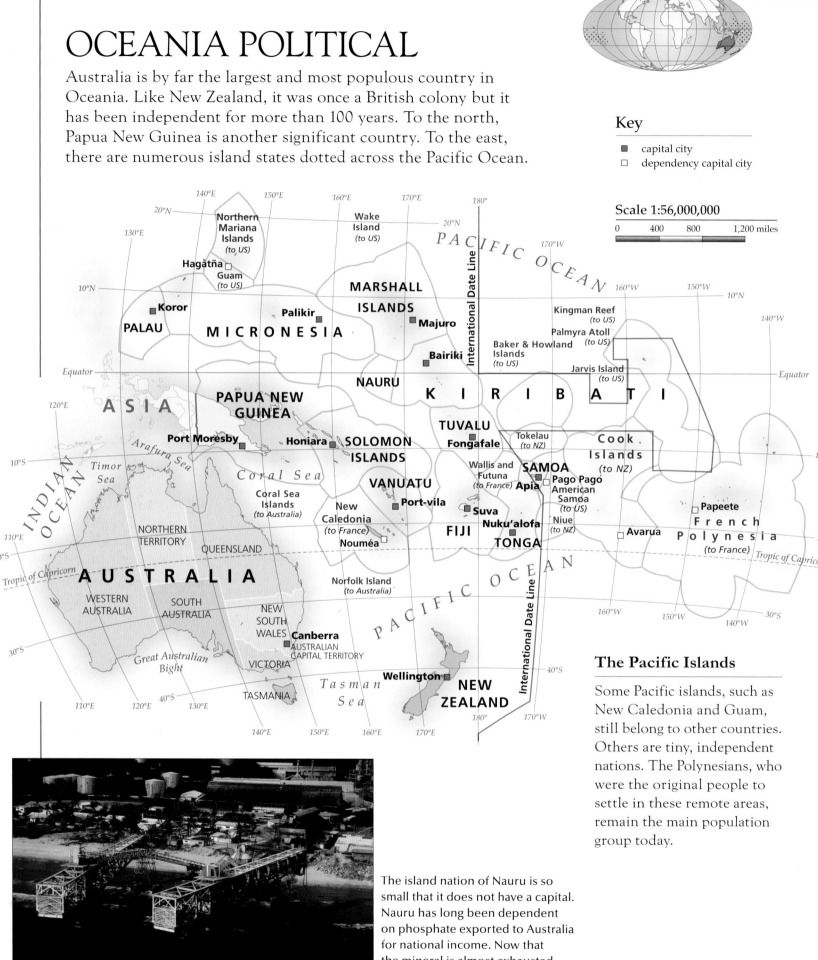

The Pacific Islands

Some Pacific islands, such as New Caledonia and Guam, still belong to other countries. Others are tiny, independent nations. The Polynesians, who were the original people to settle in these remote areas, remain the main population group today.

The island nation of Nauru is so small that it does not have a capital. Nauru has long been dependent on phosphate exported to Australia for national income. Now that the mineral is almost exhausted, Nauruans must find another way of securing their financial future.

OCEANIA PHYSICAL

Oceania is the smallest continent. It is made of up Australia, New Zealand, Papua New Guinea, and more than 20,000 small Pacific islands. Most of Oceania lies within the Tropics. Although surrounded by water, Australia is famous for its deserts. New Zealand and New Guinea have mountainous landscapes. Many of the small islands are ancient volcanoes that have sunk back into the sea and are now only a few yards above sea level.

OCEANIA FACTS

HIGHEST MOUNTAIN: Mount Wilhelm 14,793 ft

LONGEST RIVER: Murray/Darling 2,310 miles

BIGGEST LAKE: Lake Eyre 3,475 sq miles

BIGGEST ISLAND: New Guinea 308,882 sq miles

BIGGEST DESERT: Great Victoria Desert 163,862 sq miles

BIGGEST COUNTRY: Australia 2,967,909 sq miles

SMALLEST COUNTRY: Nauru 8 sq miles

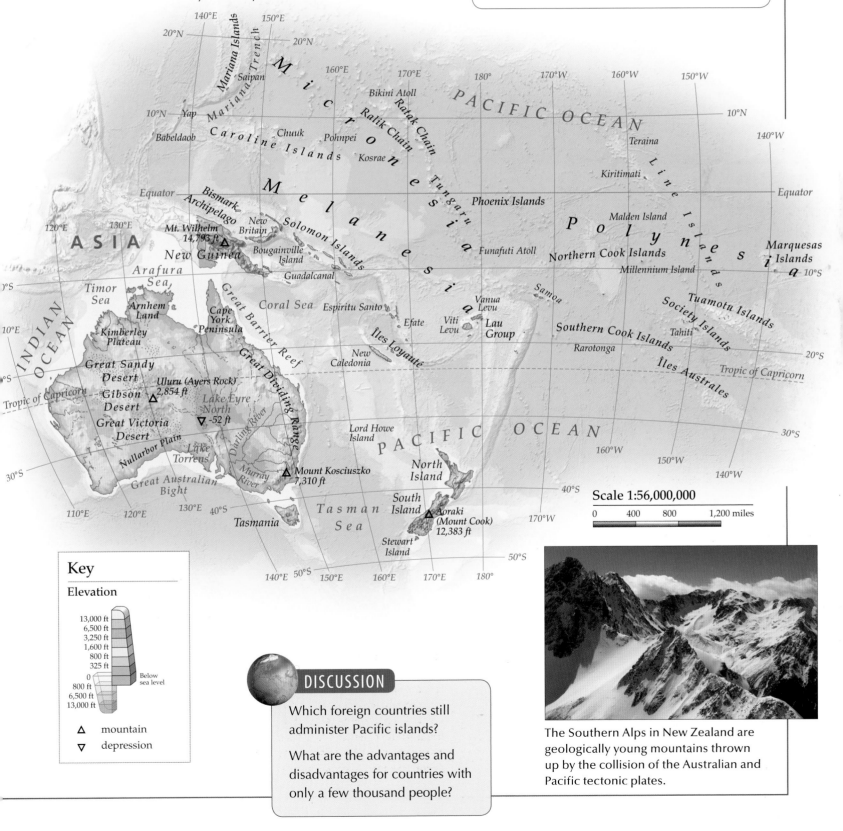

Scale 1:56,000,000

0   400   800   1,200 miles

Key

Elevation

13,000 ft
6,500 ft
3,250 ft
1,600 ft
800 ft
325 ft
0
800 ft — Below sea level
6,500 ft
13,000 ft

△ mountain
▽ depression

DISCUSSION

Which foreign countries still administer Pacific islands?

What are the advantages and disadvantages for countries with only a few thousand people?

The Southern Alps in New Zealand are geologically young mountains thrown up by the collision of the Australian and Pacific tectonic plates.

OCEANIA FROM THE SKY

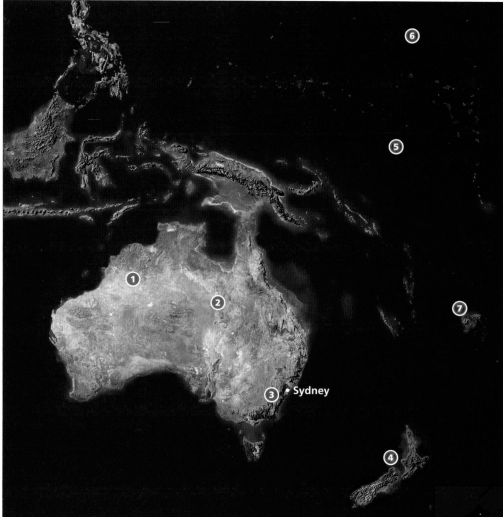

Sydney

Environmental hot spots

1 Desertification, Australia, ongoing

2 Air pollution, Mount Isa mine, Australia, ongoing

3 Bush fires, New South Wales, Australia, 2001, 2002, 2004

4 Ozone hole, New Zealand, 1980s onward

5 Soil contamination and vegetation loss, Phosphate mines, Nauru, 1908 onward

6 Nuclear test site, Bikini Atoll, Marshall Islands, 1940s and 1950s

7 Degraded coral reefs, Fiji, ongoing

The deserts and shallow coastal areas around Australia are a striking feature in this satellite image. The mountains and forests of New Guinea are clearly shown to the north.

Oceania at night

Except for Antarctica, Oceania is the least populous continent. This night image shows great empty areas in Australia and New Guinea. The main settlements are all on the coastline.

Nuclear tests

March 26, 1954

The United States, France, and Britain have all conducted nuclear testing in the remote Pacific Islands. The most famous site, Bikini Atoll, was used in the 1940s and 1950s and still suffers high levels of background radiation.

Sydney Harbor

Town Hall

Darling Harbor

Royal Botanic Gardens

Government House

Sydney Opera House

Docks

Sydney Harbor Bridge

July 2000

This aerial view shows the central business district of Sydney. It has developed around the first European settlement, which was founded in 1778.

Coral island, Kiribati

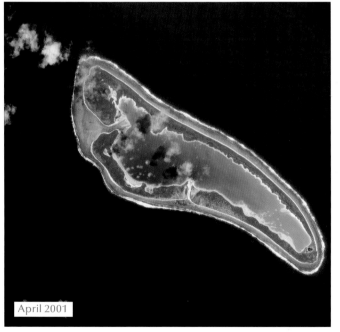

April 2001

Coral islands are scattered across the Pacific Ocean. The color of the water shows the difference between the shallow lagoon and deep surrounding ocean. Being a few feet high, coral islands are vulnerable to rising sea levels.

Bush fires

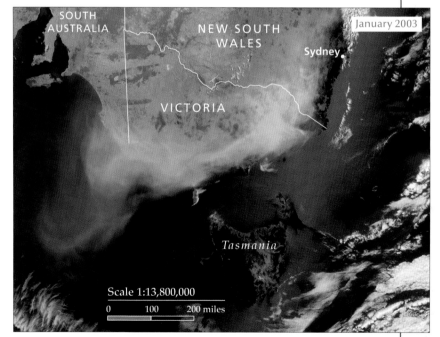

SOUTH AUSTRALIA

NEW SOUTH WALES

January 2003

Sydney

VICTORIA

Tasmania

Scale 1:13,800,000

0   100   200 miles

At the end of 2002, bush fires broke out in New South Wales, Australia, after a prolonged period of drought. At one time, there were as many as 85 fires with flames up to 100 ft high, fanned by strong winds.

AUSTRALIA AND NEW ZEALAND

Australia is the sixth largest country in the world. Deserts and scrubland cover much of the center (or outback) of the island. Along the eastern coast, the Great Dividing Range forms the most mountainous area of Australia. The majority of Australians have settled in this area. Some 1,200 miles farther east, New Zealand is one of the world's most isolated countries. It is divided into two main islands. The North Island is volcanic and the South Island is dominated by the Southern Alps.

Sydney Opera House is one of the world's most famous buildings. With a roof like a ship's sails, it has come to represent Australia.

This atoll is one of many threatened by rising sea levels in Tuvalu (see pages 84–85). The coral, which has been growing for up to 30 million years, will die if there are sudden climate changes.

EAST TIMOR

Arafura Sea

Timor Sea

Darwin

Arnhem Land

Katherine

Gulf of Car

Wyndham

NORTHERN TERRITORY

Broome

Halls Creek

Tanami Desert

Tennant Cree

Kimberley Plateau

Great Sandy Desert

Lake Mackay

Macdonnell Ranges

Alice Springs

Dampier

Exmouth

Hamersley Range

Newman

A U S T R A

Tropic of Capricorn

△ Uluru (Ayers Rock) 2,854 ft

Simps Dese

Carnarvon

Musgrave Ranges

WESTERN AUSTRALIA

SOUTH AUSTRAL

Lake Eyre North

Mount Magnet

Great Victoria Desert

Coober P

Geraldton

Reid

Kalgoorlie

Nullabor Plain

Port Augusta

Eucla

Ceduna

Great Australian Bight

Peterbor

Perth

Merredin

Fremantle

Esperance

Port Lincoln

Adela

Augusta

Albany

WHAT IS AN ATOLL?

Dense colonies of coral grow in the shallow waters around the islands of the South Pacific. Over time the coral builds up into reefs, creating lagoons around the coast. Sometimes the land sinks back into the sea, due to erosion or changes in the seabed, and the lagoon is left behind. This is known as an atoll.

PAPUA NEW GUINEA

INDONESIA

Central Range
Madang
Mount Hagen
△ Mount Wilhelm 14,793 ft
Lae
New Guinea
Kerema
Port Moresby

Rabaul
New Ireland
New Britain

Bougainville Island

Solomon Sea

Scale 1:20,000,000
(projection: Lambert Azimuthal Equal Area)

0   200   400   600 miles

1 inch on the map represents 316 miles on the ground

Solomon Islands

Honiara
Guadalcanal

SOLOMON ISLANDS

Banks Islands

Espiritu Santo

VANUATU

Port Vila

FIJI

Lautoka
Viti Levu   **Suva**
Lau Group

Cooktown
Mitchell
Cairns
Burketown
Townsville
Cloncurry
Charters Towers
Mackay
QUEENSLAND
Clermont
Longreach
Rockhampton
I A
Bundaberg
Charleville
Roma
Cunnamulla
Toowoomba
Brisbane
Surfers Paradise
Moree
Grafton
Bourke
Darling
Tamworth
Marree
NEW SOUTH WALES
Port Macquarie
Ivanhoe
Newcastle
Mildura
Parramatta
Sydney
Wagga Wagga
Wollongong
Murray
Canberra
VICTORIA
AUSTRALIAN CAPITAL TERRITORY
Horsham
△ Mount Kosciuszko 7,310 ft
Bendigo
Cooma
Mount Gambier
Melbourne
Traralgon
Geelong

Great Barrier Reef
Great Dividing Range
Great Dividing Range

Coral Sea

New Caledonia
(to France)

Îles Loyaute

New Caledonia

Nouméa

Tropic of Capricorn

Lord Howe Island

PACIFIC OCEAN

Bass Strait
Marrawah
Devonport
Launceston
TASMANIA
Tasmania
Hobart

Tasman Sea

NEW ZEALAND

Auckland
North Island   Manurewa
Hamilton   Rotorua
New Plymouth
Lake Taupo
Palmerston North   Hastings
Wellington

Aoraki (Mt. Cook) 12,283 ft △
South Island   *Southern Alps*   Christchurch

Invercargill
Stewart Island   Dunedin

Key

Elevation

13,000 ft
6,500 ft
3,250 ft
1,600 ft
800 ft
325 ft
0
800 ft
6,500 ft
13,000 ft

Below sea level

△   mountain

Settlements

⊙   over 1 million
◎   500,000 to 1 million
⊡   100,000 to 500,000
□   below 100,000

A red square indicates a national capital

ANTARCTICA

Antarctica is the fifth largest continent. Surrounded by oceans and covered by a great sheet of ice up to 10,000 ft thick, it is the last great wilderness on Earth. In winter, pack ice forms round the coast, doubling the size of the continent. The intense cold helps to drive the world's climate.

Key

ice sheet covering land

0
800 ft
6,500 ft
13,000 ft
sea depth

△ mountain
△ volcano
● research station

◇ ◇ ◇ ◇ limit of winter pack ice
⋯⋯⋯ limit of summer pack ice

Antarctic exploration
● ● ● ● Ernest Shackleton (British) 1907–8
● ● ● ● Roald Amundsen (Norwegian) 1910–12
● ● ● ● Robert Scott (British) 1910–13
● ● ● ● British Commonwealth Transantarctic 1958

SOUTHERN OCEAN

South Orkney Islands
Orcadas (to Argentina)
Signy (to UK)
Scotia Sea
Antarctic Circle
Sanae (to South Africa)
Georg von Neumayer (to Germany)
Maitri (to India)
Novolazarevskaya (to Russian Federation)
Dronning Maud Land
Asuka (to Japan)
Syowa (to Japan)
Molodezhnaya (to Russian Federation)
Enderby Land

General Bernardo O'Higgins (to Chile)
Esperanza (to Argentina)
Capitán Arturo Prat (to Chile)
Marambio (to Argentina)
Palmer (to US)
Faraday (to UK)
Halley (to UK)
Coats Land
Mount Victor 8,491 ft
Mawson (to Australia)

Weddell Sea
Belgrano II (to Argentina)
Mount Menzies 11,007 ft
Cape Darnley
Mackenzie Bay

Rothera (to UK)
San Martin (to Argentina)
Antarctic Peninsula
Filchner Ice Shelf
Berkner Island
Lambert Glacier
Zhongshan (to China)
Davis (to Australia)

Larsen Ice Shelf
Alexander Island
Ronne Ice Shelf

Bellingshausen Sea
Peter I Island (to Norway)
Thurston Island
Ellsworth Land
Vinson Massif 16,066 ft
South Pole
Amundsen-Scott (to US)

ANTARCTICA

Greater Antarctica
Davis Sea
Mirny (to Russian Federation)

Amundsen Sea
Lesser Antarctica
Transantarctic Mountains
Vostok (to Russian Federation)
South Geomagnetic Pole

Mount Sidley 13,717 ft
Wilkes Land
Vincennes Bay

SOUTHERN OCEAN
Russkaya (to Russian Federation)
Roosevelt Island
Ross Ice Shelf
McMurdo Base (to US)
Casey (to Australia)

Scott Base (to NZ)
Mount Erebus 12,448 ft
Victoria Land

Ross Sea
George V Land
Dumont d'Urville (to France)

Cape Adare
Mount Minto 13,658 ft
Leningradskaya (to Russian Federation)
Dumont d'Urville Sea
Antarctic Circle

The Antarctic Treaty

Under the terms of the 1961 Treaty, Antarctica has been set aside for scientific research. However, the continent is rich in minerals, especially oil, iron, and coal. Ensuring that Antarctica remains a world park is one of the challenges for the future.

Scale 1:29,500,000
(projection: Lambert Azimuthal Equal Area)

0   250   500   750 miles

1 inch on the map represents 466 miles on the ground

THE ARCTIC

Whereas Antarctica is a major land mass, the Arctic consists of a relatively shallow ocean. In summer, the water attracts whales, seals, and other creatures searching for food. In winter, the cold increases and pack ice extends southward across the Arctic Circle.

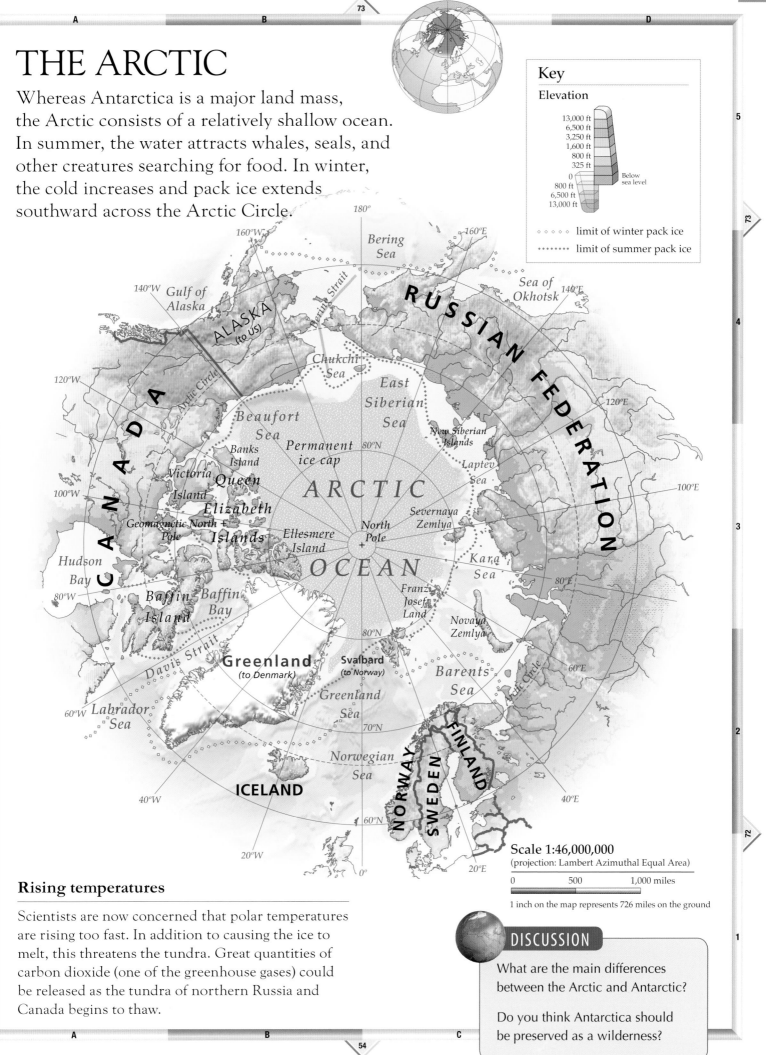

Key

Elevation

13,000 ft
6,500 ft
3,250 ft
1,600 ft
800 ft
325 ft
0
800 ft   Below sea level
6,500 ft
13,000 ft

◇ ◇ ◇ ◇ ◇   limit of winter pack ice
∙∙∙∙∙∙   limit of summer pack ice

180°
160°W   Bering Sea   160°E
140°W Gulf of Alaska   Sea of Okhotsk   140°E
ALASKA (to US)
Bering Strait
Chukchi Sea   East Siberian Sea
120°W   120°E
New Siberian Islands
Beaufort Sea
Banks Island   Permanent ice cap   80°N   Laptev Sea
Victoria Island   ARCTIC   100°E
100°W   Queen
Elizabeth   Severnaya Zemlya
Geomagnetic North Pole   Islands   North Pole
Ellesmere Island   OCEAN   Kara Sea   80°E
Hudson Bay
80°W   Franz Josef Land
Baffin Baffin   80°N   Novaya Zemlya
Island Bay   60°E
Davis Strait   Svalbard (to Norway)   Barents Sea
Greenland (to Denmark)   Arctic Circle
60°W Labrador Sea   Greenland Sea   70°N
Norwegian Sea   NORWAY SWEDEN FINLAND
40°W   ICELAND   40°E
60°N
20°W   20°E
0°

CANADA
RUSSIAN FEDERATION

Scale 1:46,000,000
(projection: Lambert Azimuthal Equal Area)

0   500   1,000 miles

1 inch on the map represents 726 miles on the ground

Rising temperatures

Scientists are now concerned that polar temperatures are rising too fast. In addition to causing the ice to melt, this threatens the tundra. Great quantities of carbon dioxide (one of the greenhouse gases) could be released as the tundra of northern Russia and Canada begins to thaw.

DISCUSSION

What are the main differences between the Arctic and Antarctic?

Do you think Antarctica should be preserved as a wilderness?

WORLD DEVELOPMENT

Development is about improving the quality of people's lives. This involves not only helping them to become richer, but also seeing that they stay healthy, have the chance to learn new things, and fulfill their potential as human beings. As human numbers continue to rise, we need to ensure that we share the earth's resources fairly and use them sustainably.

> *"We must recognize that our common humanity is more important than our differences."*
>
> Bill Clinton
> President of the United States, 1993-2001

Differences in development

The charts on the following pages show aspects of development in different countries. MEDCs are represented by the US, UK, and Russian Federation. LEDCs are represented by Brazil, Kenya, Pakistan, and China.

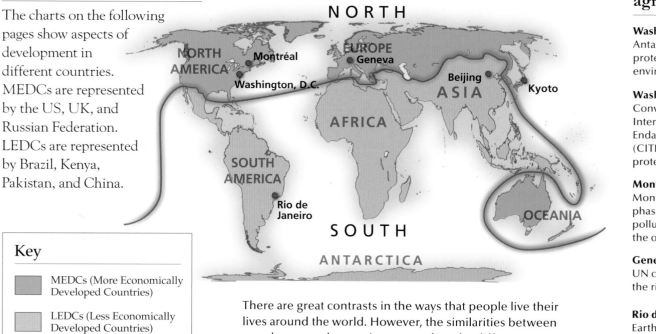

There are great contrasts in the ways that people live their lives around the world. However, the similarities between people are much more important than the differences.

Key

- ▢ MEDCs (More Economically Developed Countries)
- ▢ LEDCs (Less Economically Developed Countries)
- — North-South divide

International agreements

Washington, D.C., 1959
Antarctic Treaty protects the natural environment

Washington, D.C., 1975
Convention on International Trade in Endangered Species (CITES) attempts to protect wildlife

Montréal, 1987
Montréal Protocol phases out CFCs and pollutants that damage the ozone layer

Geneva, 1989
UN convention on the rights of the child

Rio de Janeiro, 1992
Earth summit sets an environmental agenda for the 21st century

Beijing, 1995
UN conference on human rights recognizes the status of women

Kyoto, 1997
Convention on climate change agrees international limits on carbon emissions

The world family

Find out more about the human family from this illustration. The figures tell you how many of us would belong to each group if there were only 100 people in the world.

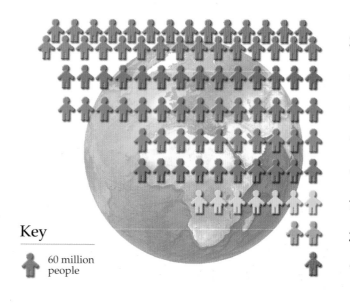

29 are under 15 years old

14 do not have enough to eat

14 are unable to read or write

10 have a car

10 use the Internet

7 are over 65 years old

2 have never been to school

1 is a refugee or slave

Key

👤 60 million people

DISCUSSION

What goals would you set to improve life in your own school or community?

On a global scale, do you think that the North-South divide will become more or less important in the future?

Millennium Development Goals

In 2000, 189 member countries of the United Nations agreed on a set of goals to reduce poverty and improve people's lives around the world by 2015.

You can find out more about human welfare in the next few pages (94–103). As you make comparisons, remember that there are many inequalities within countries as well as between them.

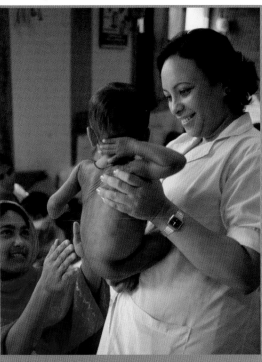

Goals 4, 5, and 6 Cut the number of deaths from disease and childbirth.

Goal 1 Eradicate extreme poverty and hunger.

Goal 7 See that the environment is used sustainably.

Goal 2 See that all children go to elementary school.

Goal 3 Promote equality between men and women.

Goal 8 Develop partnerships between nations.

HEALTH

Millennium development targets:

- Reduce the number of children who die under the age of 5 by two-thirds
- Halt the spread of AIDS and malaria

In many parts of the world, people are living longer than they used to. People are healthier as a result of improvements in food and water supply. There are also more doctors and hospitals to help them when they become sick. Around the world, rich people generally live longer than those who are poor. In eastern Europe and central Asia, economic problems have affected people's health. AIDS has led to a sharp fall in life expectancy in sub-Saharan Africa.

① USA

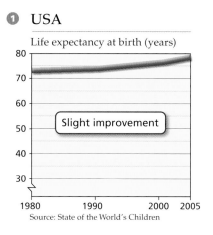

Life expectancy at birth (years)

Slight improvement

Source: State of the World's Children

Population pyramids

Kenya

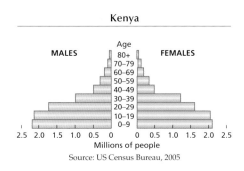

Source: US Census Bureau, 2005

There are many young people in Kenya, as indicated by the triangular shape of this pyramid.

Russian Federation

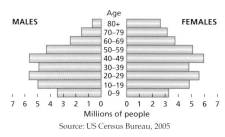

Source: US Census Bureau, 2005

The difference in the number of men and women over 60 is the result of World War II.

USA

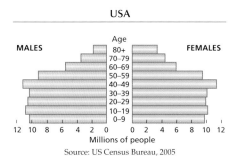

Source: US Census Bureau, 2005

This more regular profile suggests that the US has an aging population.

China

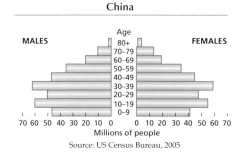

Source: US Census Bureau, 2005

In China, the One Child Policy has led to a drop in the number of children under the age of 10.

⑤ Brazil

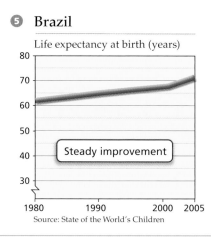

Life expectancy at birth (years)

Steady improvement

Source: State of the World's Children

② UK

Life expectancy at birth (years)

Slight improvement

Source: State of the World's Children

③ Russian Federation

Life expectancy at birth (years)

Problems in 1990s with break up of Soviet Union

Source: State of the World's Children

Improvements in healthcare mean that this Chinese child can expect to live until the last decades of this century.

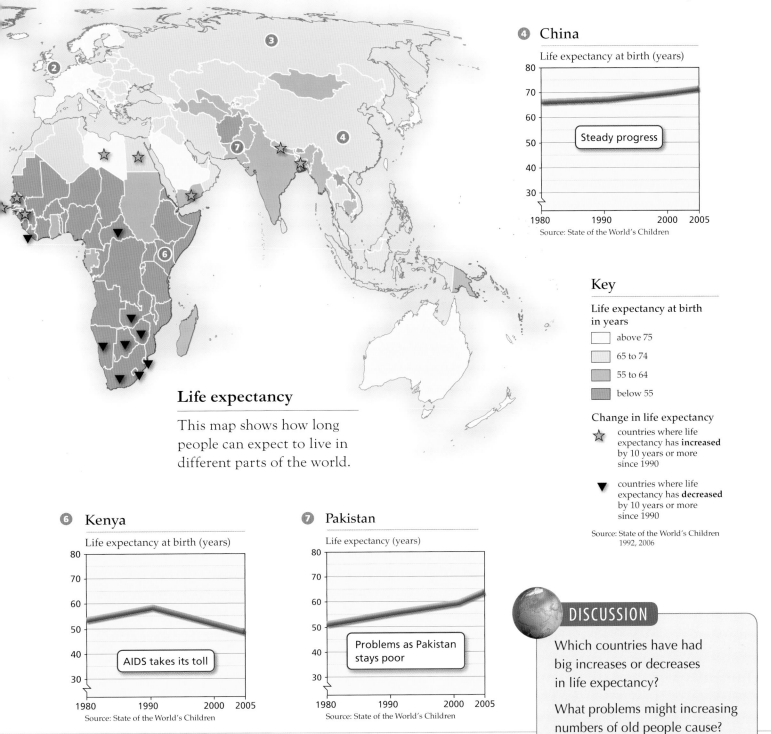

④ China

Life expectancy at birth (years)

Steady progress

Source: State of the World's Children

Life expectancy

This map shows how long people can expect to live in different parts of the world.

Key

Life expectancy at birth in years

☐ above 75

☐ 65 to 74

☐ 55 to 64

☐ below 55

Change in life expectancy

☆ countries where life expectancy has **increased** by 10 years or more since 1990

▼ countries where life expectancy has **decreased** by 10 years or more since 1990

Source: State of the World's Children 1992, 2006

⑥ Kenya

Life expectancy at birth (years)

AIDS takes its toll

Source: State of the World's Children

⑦ Pakistan

Life expectancy (years)

Problems as Pakistan stays poor

Source: State of the World's Children

DISCUSSION

Which countries have had big increases or decreases in life expectancy?

What problems might increasing numbers of old people cause?

WEALTH

Millennium development target:

Halve the number of people earning less than $1 a day

The world's wealth is distributed unevenly. In every country there are some people who are very rich and others who are very poor. Globally, there are a few countries that are much richer than the rest. This leaves 80% of the world's population with less than 20% of the world's wealth.

Wealth worldwide

This map shows differences in wealth between countries. It is based on GDP (gross domestic product) per head. The GDP is the total value of the goods and services a country produces in a year.

Change in wealth

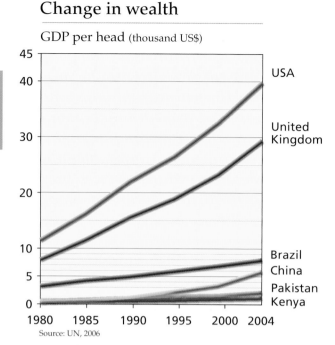

GDP per head (thousand US$)

Source: UN, 2006

Over the last 20 years, differences in wealth between nations have become steadily greater.

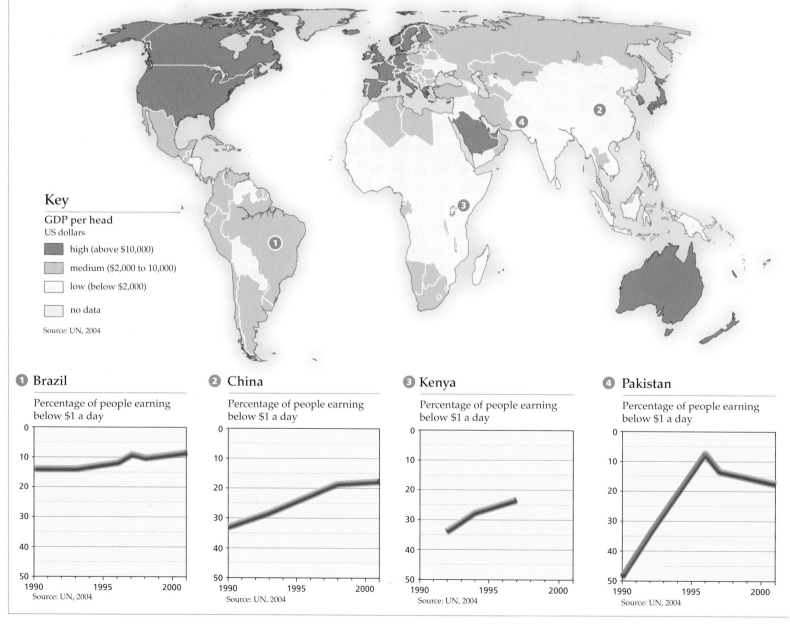

Key

GDP per head
US dollars

- high (above $10,000)
- medium ($2,000 to 10,000)
- low (below $2,000)
- no data

Source: UN, 2004

❶ Brazil

Percentage of people earning below $1 a day

Source: UN, 2004

❷ China

Percentage of people earning below $1 a day

Source: UN, 2004

❸ Kenya

Percentage of people earning below $1 a day

Source: UN, 2004

❹ Pakistan

Percentage of people earning below $1 a day

Source: UN, 2004

FOOD

Millennium development target:

Halve the number of people who suffer from hunger

Around the world some people have too much to eat, others have too little. Malnutrition has a particularly severe effect on young children. Not only are they weaker than adults, they can also suffer permanent brain damage if not properly fed. What happens in the first few years sets the stage for success in later life.

World food consumption

Key

Daily calorie intake per person

- below 2,000 – less than 90% of requirements
- 2,000 to 2,500 – 90 to 100%
- 2,500 to 3,000 – 101 to 110%
- above 3,000 – over 110%
- no data
- ▼ countries where many young children are underweight

Source: Human Development Report, 2004

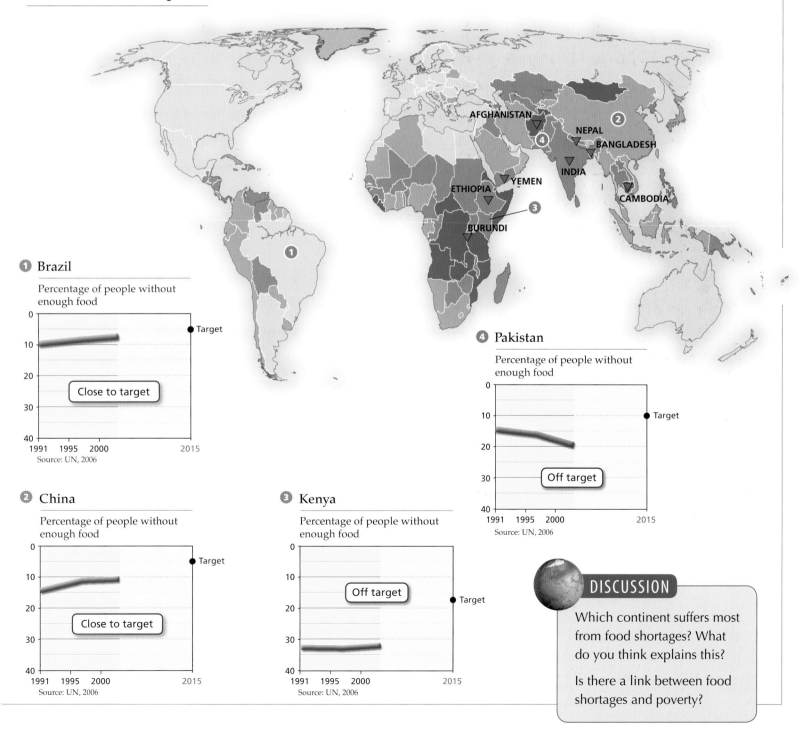

① Brazil

Percentage of people without enough food

● Target

Close to target

1991 1995 2000   2015
Source: UN, 2006

④ Pakistan

Percentage of people without enough food

● Target

Off target

1991 1995 2000   2015
Source: UN, 2006

② China

Percentage of people without enough food

● Target

Close to target

1991 1995 2000   2015
Source: UN, 2006

③ Kenya

Percentage of people without enough food

Off target

● Target

1991 1995 2000   2015
Source: UN, 2006

DISCUSSION

Which continent suffers most from food shortages? What do you think explains this?

Is there a link between food shortages and poverty?

EDUCATION

Millennium development target:

Ensure that all children, boys and girls alike, finish their course at elementary school

"There is no single more effective antipoverty strategy than education."

Gordon Brown,
UK politician

In the modern world, it is essential to know how to read and write. Education also helps people to live more fulfilling lives. All over the world the number of pupils attending school is improving. However, 140 million children still have no access to education. Many of them live in south Asia and sub-Saharan Africa. Girls suffer more than boys since they are expected to do jobs around the house. This has an impact in later life. Educated women tend to have fewer children and look after their families better than those who have not been to school.

Children in elementary school

This map shows the percentage of children from different countries who have completed their elementary education.

① Brazil

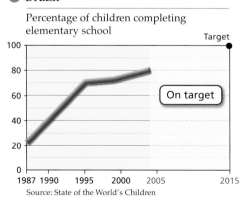

Percentage of children completing elementary school

Source: State of the World's Children

② Kenya

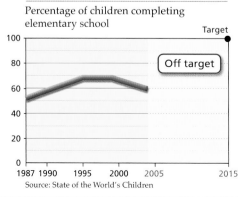

Percentage of children completing elementary school

Source: State of the World's Children

③ Pakistan

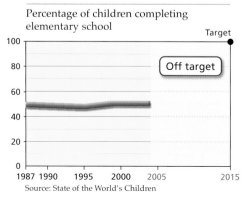

Percentage of children completing elementary school

Source: State of the World's Children

Differences between boys and girls

Average number of years schooling for boys and girls

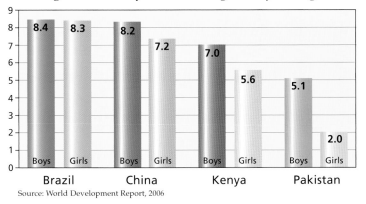

Brazil — Boys 8.4, Girls 8.3
China — Boys 8.2, Girls 7.2
Kenya — Boys 7.0, Girls 5.6
Pakistan — Boys 5.1, Girls 2.0

Source: World Development Report, 2006

In most countries, boys have priority for schooling.

Differences between towns and villages

Average number of years schooling in urban and rural areas

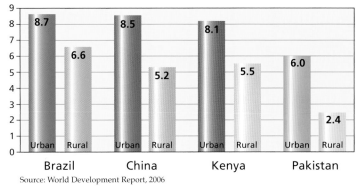

Brazil — Urban 8.7, Rural 6.6
China — Urban 8.5, Rural 5.2
Kenya — Urban 8.1, Rural 5.5
Pakistan — Urban 6.0, Rural 2.4

Source: World Development Report, 2006

Children living in urban areas have a better chance of going to school than those in rural areas.

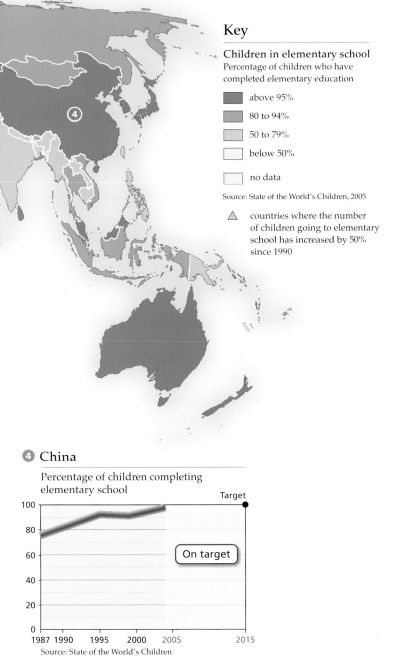

Key

Children in elementary school
Percentage of children who have completed elementary education

- above 95%
- 80 to 94%
- 50 to 79%
- below 50%
- no data

Source: State of the World's Children, 2005

△ countries where the number of children going to elementary school has increased by 50% since 1990

Adult illiteracy

Percentage of adult population who can read and write

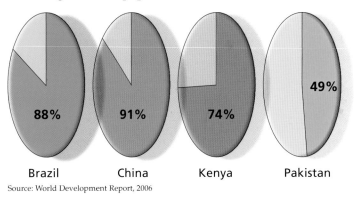

Brazil 88% China 91% Kenya 74% Pakistan 49%

Source: World Development Report, 2006

There are 860 million illiterate adults worldwide—two-thirds of them are women.

④ China

Percentage of children completing elementary school

Target — On target

1987 1990 1995 2000 2005 ... 2015

Source: State of the World's Children

DISCUSSION

Why do you think children in poor countries have a better chance of going to school in towns than in villages?

How would your life be affected if you were unable to read and write?

WATER

Millennium development target:

Halve the number of people without safe water and sanitation

Water is essential for our lives. We use it for drinking, washing, cooking and cleaning. In poor countries (LEDCs), obtaining clean water can be a problem. The people who live in shanty towns around big cities often have to make do with polluted supplies. In some parts of rural Africa and Asia, women spend many hours each day simply fetching and carrying water of often poor quality from a pump or well.

Eighty percent of sickness and disease in LEDCs is caused by dirty water and poor sanitation. Nearly all these illnesses could be prevented. It would cost relatively little to bring safe water to everyone. This would help to save the lives of thousands of young children who die needlessly from waterborne diseases every day.

"No single measure would do more to reduce disease and save lives in the developing world than bringing safe water and adequate sanitation to all."

Kofi Annan, former UN Secretary General

Safe drinking water

This map shows the number of people who have access to clean water around the world.

Key

Access to clean drinking water
(% of population)

- 90 to 100
- 75 to 89
- 50 to 74
- below 50

- no data

Source: UN, 2004

Water disputes

- ☆ conflict over access to water
- ⌒ disputed river

BRAZIL, ARGENTI
Paraná River

It costs around $30 per person to provide safe water and sanitation in deprived areas. Everyone in the community benefits from the improvements.

❶ Brazil

Percentage of population with access to clean water

Target

Ahead of target

1990   2004   2015

Source: UN, 2007

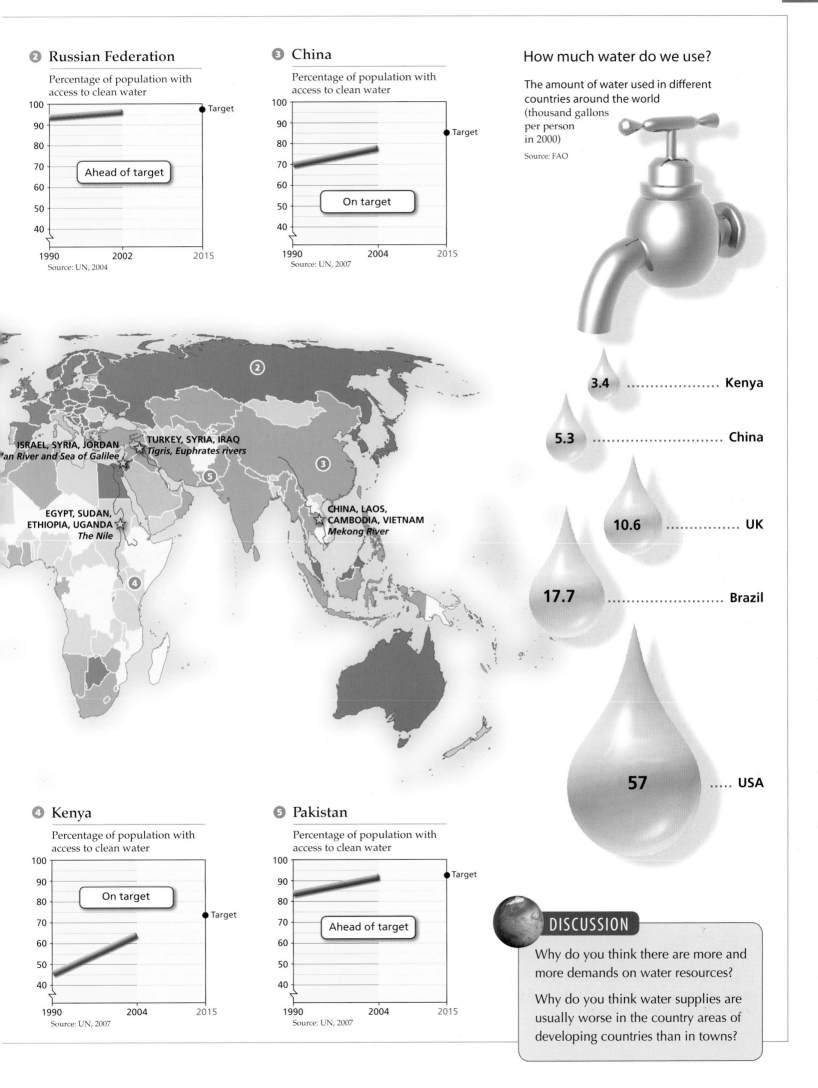

❷ Russian Federation

Percentage of population with access to clean water

Ahead of target

Target

1990 2002 2015

Source: UN, 2004

❸ China

Percentage of population with access to clean water

On target

Target

1990 2004 2015

Source: UN, 2007

How much water do we use?

The amount of water used in different countries around the world (thousand gallons per person in 2000)

Source: FAO

3.4 .... Kenya

5.3 .... China

10.6 .... UK

17.7 .... Brazil

57 ..... USA

ISRAEL, SYRIA, JORDAN
an River and Sea of Galilee

TURKEY, SYRIA, IRAQ
Tigris, Euphrates rivers

EGYPT, SUDAN, ETHIOPIA, UGANDA
The Nile

CHINA, LAOS, CAMBODIA, VIETNAM
Mekong River

❹ Kenya

Percentage of population with access to clean water

On target

Target

1990 2004 2015

Source: UN, 2007

❺ Pakistan

Percentage of population with access to clean water

Ahead of target

Target

1990 2004 2015

Source: UN, 2007

DISCUSSION

Why do you think there are more and more demands on water resources?

Why do you think water supplies are usually worse in the country areas of developing countries than in towns?

ENVIRONMENT

Millennium development target:
Reverse the loss of environmental resources

Like all other living creatures, our survival depends on the natural environment. Water, air, food, and fuel are essential for our daily lives. We also have to dispose of waste and garbage. The amount of land needed to sustain us is known as our "environmental footprint."

The growth in human numbers and the increasing demand for resources mean our environmental footprint is growing heavier. We now use more resources each year than the earth can naturally replace. Reversing this trend is a key challenge for the future.

> *"The greatest challenge of ...our time... is to save the planet from destruction. It will require changing the very foundations of modern civilization— the relationship of humans to nature."*
>
> Mikhail Gorbachev
> President of the Soviet Union, 1985–1991

Environmental footprints

This map shows the amount of land used by people in different countries.

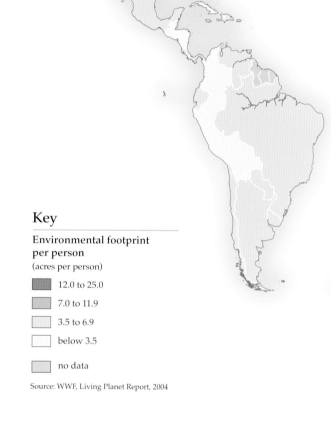

Key

Environmental footprint
per person
(acres per person)

- 12.0 to 25.0
- 7.0 to 11.9
- 3.5 to 6.9
- below 3.5
- no data

Source: WWF, Living Planet Report, 2004

World footprint

Number of Earths required to support human activity

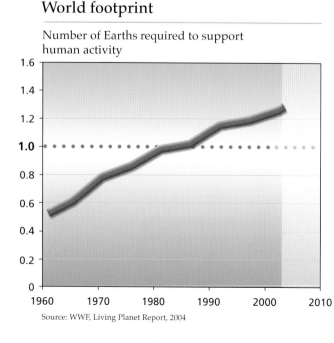

1960   1970   1980   1990   2000   2010

Source: WWF, Living Planet Report, 2004

Since the mid 1980s the demands that people have placed on the earth have exceeded its natural capacity.

DISCUSSION

Is it fair that some countries have a much larger environmental footprint than others?

What could you do to reduce the size of your environmental footprint?

Renewable energy is one way of changing the demands we place on the environment. Cutting our consumption is also essential, especially in Europe and North America.

Country footprints

In some countries, people make much bigger demands on the environment than others. These footprints were calculated by dividing the amount of land needed to provide what each country uses by its total population.

(acres per person)
Source: WWF Living Planet Report, 2004

Earth's capacity

(5.4 acres per person)

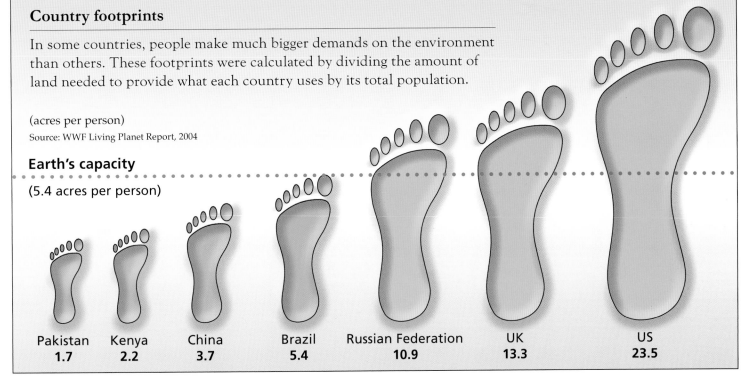

Pakistan	Kenya	China	Brazil	Russian Federation	UK	US
1.7	2.2	3.7	5.4	10.9	13.3	23.5

COUNTRY FACTFILE

This table provides data about geography and development in countries with a population of more than 30 million people.

	Area (sq miles)	Population (million)	GNI per capita ($US)	Life expectancy at birth	Adult literacy rate male	female	Carbon emissions (tons per capita)
Afghanistan	230,000	30	-	43	51	21	-
Algeria	920,000	33	1,890	70	76	57	5.6
Argentina	1,080,000	40	3,650	74	97	97	3.7
Bangladesh	40,000	142	400	62	49	30	0.3
Brazil	3,280,000	186	2,710	68	87	87	1.8
Canada	3,860,000	32	23,930	79	-	-	19.7
China	3,860,000	1,316	1,100	71	92	78	3.5
Colombia	380,000	46	1,810	72	92	92	1.4
Congo, Dem. Rep.	770,000	58	640	48	73	50	0.4
Egypt	380,000	74	1,390	69	67	44	2.2
Ethiopia	380,000	76	90	46	47	31	0.1
France	230,000	60	24,770	79	-	-	6.8
Germany	150,000	83	25,250	78	-	-	10.8
India	1,150,000	1,103	530	64	68	45	1.3
Indonesia	770,000	223	810	67	92	82	1.5
Iran	770,000	70	2,000	70	83	69	6.2
Italy	120,000	58	21,560	79	-	-	8.5
Japan	150,000	128	34,510	82	-	-	10.7
Kenya	230,000	34	390	44	89	76	0.3
Korea (South)	380,000	48	12,030	76	-	-	10.6
Mexico	770,000	107	6,230	74	93	89	4.4
Morocco	150,000	31	1,320	69	62	36	1.3
Myanmar	230,000	47	-	57	89	81	0.2
Nigeria	340,000	132	320	51	72	56	0.4
Pakistan	270,000	158	470	61	57	28	0.9
Philippines	120,000	83	1,080	70	95	95	1.1
Poland	120,000	39	5,270	74	-	-	8.7
Russian Federation	6,560,000	143	2,610	67	100	99	11.4
South Africa	380,000	47	2,780	47	86	85	7.9
Spain	190,000	43	16,990	79	-	-	8.0
Sudan	1,150,000	36	460	56	69	46	0.3
Tanzania	380,000	39	290	43	84	67	0.1
Thailand	190,000	64	2,190	69	97	94	4.3
Turkey	300,000	73	2,790	71	93	77	3.4
Ukraine	230,000	46	970	70	100	100	7.3
United Kingdom	70,000	60	28,350	78	-	-	10.4
United States	380,000	298	37,610	77	-	-	21.8
Vietnam	120,000	84	480	69	95	91	1.0

HOW TO USE THIS INDEX

To find a place in the atlas first look up the name in the index. Next to the name you will see a page number and grid reference, e.g. Canary Islands **64 B4**. Use the page number to go to the correct page in the atlas, page **64** in this example. Next look along the bottom of the page to find the letter **B** and then at the side of the page to find the number **4**. You will find the Canary Islands where these two references meet.

The index also tells you the latitude and longitude of places, e.g. Canary Islands 64 B4 **28°0'N 15°30'W**. This reference is used to find the exact position of a place on the surface of the earth. You can see how latitude and longitude works by looking at pages 6 and 7 of the atlas.

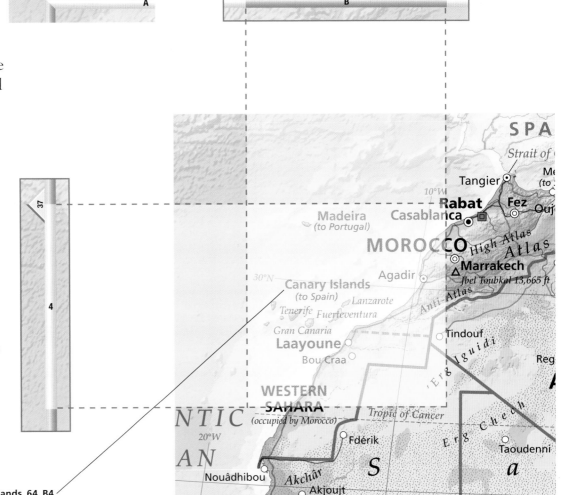

Canary Islands 64 B4

A

Aalborg	55 B2	57°3'N 9°56'E
Aberdeen	56 D5	57°10'N 2°4'W
Abha	75 E1	18°16'N 42°32'E
Abidjan	64 C2	5°19'N 4°1'W
Abilene	37 E2	32°27'N 99°44'W
Abu Dhabi	75 F2	24°30'N 54°20'E
Abuja	64 D2	9°4'N 7°28'E
Acapulco	38 B2	16°51'N 99°53'W
Accra	64 C2	5°33'N 0°15'W
Aconcagua, Cerro	49 B3	32°36'S 69°53'W
A Coruña	56 C2	43°22'N 8°24'W
Adamawa Highlands	64 D2	7°0'N 12°0'E
Adana	74 D4	37°0'N 35°19'E
Addis Ababa	65 G2	9°0'N 38°43'E
Adelaide	88 D2	34°56'S 138°36'E
Aden	75 E1	12°51'N 45°5'E
Aden, Gulf of	65 H2	12°22'N 46°51'E
Adriatic Sea	57 F2	43°32'N 14°34'E
Afghanistan	72 C1	32°39'N 64°23'E
Agra	77 E4	27°9'N 78°0'E
Ahaggar	64 D3	23°54'N 6°23'E
Ahmadabad	76 D3	23°3'N 72°40'E
Ahvaz	75 F3	31°20'N 48°38'E
Aïr, Massif de l'	64 D3	18°25'N 8°55'E
Akchâr	64 B3	20°54'N 14°11'W
Akita	81 F4	39°44'N 140°6'E
Aktau	72 C2	43°37'N 51°14'E
Aktobe	72 C3	50°18'N 57°10'E
Alabama	37 G3	33°6'N 86°44'W
Alabama River	37 G2	31°8'N 87°57'W
Aland Islands	55 D3	60°14'N 19°54'E
Aland Sea	55 D3	60°0'N 20°0'E
Alaska	36 A4	65°0'N 150°0'W
Alaska, Gulf of	34 B2	58°0'N 145°0'W
Alaska Peninsula	36 A3	57°0'N 158°0'W

Alaska Range	36 A3	63°0'N 150°0'W
Albania	59 A2	41°12'N 19°58'E
Albany, Australia	88 C2	35°3'S 117°54'E
Albany, Canada	35 E1	51°15'N 84°6'W
Albany, USA	37 H4	42°39'N 73°45'W
Alberta	34 C2	55°33'N 114°38'W
Albert, Lake	67 E5	1°41'N 30°55'E
Albuquerque	36 D3	35°5'N 106°38'W
Aleppo	74 D4	36°14'N 37°10'E
Aleutian Islands	36 A3	52°0'N 176°0'W
Alexandria	65 F4	31°7'N 29°51'E
Al Fujayrah	75 G3	25°9'N 56°18'E
Algeria	64 C4	28°4'N 0°45'E
Algiers	64 D5	36°47'N 2°58'E
Al Hufuf	75 F3	25°21'N 49°34'E
Alice Springs	88 D3	23°42'S 133°52'E
Al Lādhiqīyah	74 D4	35°31'N 35°47'E
Allahabad	77 E4	25°27'N 81°50'E
Almaty	72 D2	43°19'N 76°55'E
Altai Mountains	78 C4	48°0'N 88°36'E
Altun Shan	78 C3	37°20'N 87°13'E
Amarillo	37 E3	35°13'N 101°50'W
Amazon	48 B6	0°10'S 49°0'W
Amazon Basin	48 C6	4°48'S 62°44'W
Amazon, Mouths of the	48 D6	1°0'N 48°0'W
Ambon	83 F1	3°41'S 128°10'E
Amindivi Islands	76 D1	11°0'N 73°0'E
Amman	74 D3	31°57'N 35°56'E
Amol	75 F4	36°31'N 52°24'E
Amritsar	77 E5	31°38'N 74°55'E
Amsterdam	57 E4	52°22'N 4°54'E
Amundsen Gulf	34 C3	70°42'N 124°1'W
Amur	79 F5	53°10'N 124°52'E
Anadyr'	73 G5	64°41'N 177°22'E
Anadyr, Gulf of	73 G5	64°0'N 178°0'W
Anatolia	74 D5	39°43'N 44°39'E
Anchorage	36 A3	61°13'N 149°52'W

Andaman Islands	77 G2	12°12'N 92°0'E
Andaman Sea	82 C3	11°0'N 108°0'E
Andes	49 B4	2°0'N 78°0'W
Andorra	56 D2	42°34'N 1°34'E
Angel Falls	48 C6	5°52'N 62°19'W
Angola	66 D3	11°8'S 19°25'E
Anguilla	39 G3	18°26'N 63°0'W
Ankara	74 D5	39°55'N 32°50'E
An Nafud	75 E3	28°14'N 40°42'E
An Najaf	75 E3	31°59'N 44°19'E
Annapurna	77 F4	28°30'N 83°50'E
Anshan	79 F4	41°6'N 122°55'E
Antakya	74 D4	36°12'N 36°10'E
Antalya	74 C4	36°53'N 30°42'E
Antananarivo	67 G2	18°52'S 47°30'E
Antarctica	90 B3	90°0'S 0°0'E
Antigua and Barbuda	39 H2	17°21'N 61°48'W
A'nyemaqen Shan	78 D3	34°11'N 100°54'E
Aomori	81 F4	40°50'N 140°43'E
Aoraki (Mount Cook)	89 G1	43°39'S 170°5'E
Aoukâr	64 B3	18°6'N 9°28'W
Appalachian Mountains	37 G3	34°53'N 84°28'W
Arabian Peninsula	75 E2	22°22'N 44°32'E
Arabian Sea	76 D2	15°0'N 65°0'E
Arafura Sea	88 D5	9°0'S 135°0'E
Araguaia, Rio	48 D5	5°21'S 48°41'W
Aral Sea	72 C2	44°34'N 59°49'E
Ararat, Mount	75 E5	39°43'N 44°19'E
Aras	75 E5	39°18'N 45°7'E
Archangel	58 C6	64°32'N 40°40'E
Arctic Ocean	91 B3	90°0'N 0°0'E
Ardabil	75 E4	38°15'N 48°18'E
Argentina	49 B2	35°54'S 64°55'W
Argun	79 F5	50°52'N 119°31'E
Århus	55 B2	56°9'N 10°11'E
Arizona	36 D3	34°8'N 112°7'W

Arkansas	37 F3	34°56'N 92°14'W
Arkansas River	37 F3	34°N 91°19'W
Armenia	75 E5	40°36'N 44°22'E
Arnhem Land	88 D4	14°3'S 133°24'E
Aruba	39 G2	12°30'N 69°55'W
Aru, Kepulauan	83 G1	6°10'S 134°20'E
Asadabad	72 C1	34°52'N 71°9'E
Asahi-dake	81 F5	43°42'N 142°50'E
Asahikawa	81 F5	43°46'N 142°23'E
Asansol	77 F3	23°40'N 86°59'E
Aşgabat	72 C2	37°58'N 58°22'E
Asmara	65 G3	15°15'N 38°58'E
'Assal, Lac	65 G3	11°2'N 41°51'E
Astana	72 D2	51°13'N 71°25'E
Astrakhan'	59 D3	46°20'N 48°1'E
Asunción	49 C4	25°17'S 57°36'W
Aswân	65 F3	24°3'N 32°59'E
Atacama Desert	49 B4	21°39'S 69°26'W
Athabasca, Lake	34 D2	59°7'N 110°0'W
Athens	59 B2	37°59'N 23°44'E
Atka	36 A3	52°12'N 174°14'W
Atlanta	37 G3	33°45'N 84°23'W
Atlantic Ocean	10	0°0' 40°0'W
Atlas Mountains	64 C4	33°11'N 2°56'W
Atyrau	72 C2	47°7'N 51°56'E
Auckland	89 G1	36°53'S 174°46'E
Augusta	37 H5	44°20'S 69°44'W
Austin	37 E2	30°16'N 97°45'W
Australia	88 D3	25°0'S 135°0'E
Australian Capital Territory	89 E2	35°27'S 148°57'E
Austria	57 F3	47°28'N 12°31'E
Axel Heiberg Island	34 D4	79°34'N 91°16'W
Aydın	74 C4	37°51'N 27°51'E
Ayers Rock see Uluru
Azerbaijan	75 E5	41°7'N 47°10'E
Az Zahrān	75 F3	26°18'N 50°2'E

CREDITS